SEX FACTS

A HANDBOOK FOR THE CARNALLY CURIOUS

SEX FACTS

LESLEE WELCH

A Citadel Press Book
Published by Carol Publishing Group

Carol Publishing Group Edition, 1995

Previously published as *The Complete Book of Sexual Trivia*

A Citadel Press Book
Published by Carol Publishing Group
Citadel Press is a registered trademark of Carol Communications, Inc.

Editorial Offices: 600 Madison Avenue, New York, NY 10022
Sales & Distribution Offices: 120 Enterprise Avenue, Secaucus, NJ 07094
In Canada: Canadian Manda Group, One Atlantic Avenue, Suite 105
Toronto, Ontario, M6K 3E7

Queries regarding rights and permissions should be addressed to:
Carol Publishing Group, 600 Madison Avenue, New York, NY 10022

Manufactured in the United States of America
10 9 8 7 6 5 4 3 2 1

Carol Publishing Group books are available at special discounts
for bulk purchases, sales promotions, fund raising, or
educational purposes. Special editions can also be created to
specifications. For details contact: Special Sales Department,
Carol Publishing Group, 120 Enterprise Ave., Secaucus, NJ 07094

Library of Congress Cataloging-in-Publication Data

Welch, Leslee.
    Sex facts : a handbook for the carnally curious / Leslee Welch.
        p.   cm.
    "A Citadel Press book."
    ISBN 0-8065-1678-X (pbk.)
    1. Sex—Miscellanea. 2. Sex customs—Miscellanea. I. Title.
HQ25.W45   1995
306.7—dc20   95-9364
                                                          CIP

CONTENTS

INTRODUCTION

Sex, in one form or another, has been around for a long time. No other aspect of human existence has so universally occupied the hearts and minds of people throughout the ages. Evidence of sexual expression and representation can be found among artifacts dating to prehistoric man, and no subsequent eras, from periods of licentiousness to periods of sexual repression, have failed to chronicle its impact. Today, we are continually bombarded with sex, whether it be blatant or subliminal, and its influence affects everything from the clothes we wear to the food we eat.

The Complete Book of Sexual Trivia should provide an interesting cultural and historical perspective of human sexuality and its impact on our lives. Over 650 fascinating sexual facts are compiled in this book for your information and entertainment, from common biological trivia to amazing historical sex facts and bizarre sexual customs of different cultures. Included in this collection of sexual trivia are current statistical data which reflect American attitudes and sexual trends, as well as sex crime and sexually transmitted disease in the United States.

I hope you enjoy reading *The Complete Book of Sexual Trivia* and as you peruse through the following pages, discover some useful information, a bit of humor, or a few surprises.

THE SEXUAL TRIVIA CHALLENGE

How much sexual trivia do YOU know? Grab paper and pencil and test your knowledge and sexpertise by taking the Sexual Trivia Challenge. Some of the following questions are common sexual facts, while others are more difficult. You will find the answers on page 89. Good luck—and have fun!

1. The average length of the unerect flaccid penis is—
   A. 2½ inches   B. 4 inches   C. 5½ inches

2. The circumference of the erect penis is approximately—
   A. 2½ inches   B. 4 inches   C. 5½ inches

3. How many calories are there in a teaspoon of semen?
   A. 5 calories   B. 50 calories   C. none

4. How many calories are burned during intercourse?
   A. 50 calories   B. 100 calories   C. 300 calories

5. Of the 400 to 600 million sperm that are present with a single ejaculation, how many will reach the site of fertilization in the fallopian tubes?
   A. 300   B. 3,000   C. 3,000,000

6. Which country has developed an oral contraceptive for men?
   A. the United States   B. India   C. China

7. "Passion purpura" is the medical term for—
   A. a fungal infection similar to "jock itch" that is spread by sexual contact

1

B. red abrasions on wrists or ankles caused by bondage
C. a hickey

8. Phenylethylamine, a chemical produced by the brain and responsible for the ecstatic highs of love and sexual attraction, can also be found in which food?
A. passion fruit   B. oysters   C. chocolate

9. Tincture of belladonna (meaning "fair lady") was used by Italian Renaissance women to make themselves more sexually attractive and to enhance what part of the body?
A. eyes   B. lips   C. breasts

10. The word "gymnasium" has its origin in the Greek term *gymnos*, which means—
A. whorehouse   B. women's birthing place   C. naked

11. Another name for the French kiss during the nineteenth century was—
A. *maraichinage*   B. soul kiss   C. meal of tongues

12. What was the cost of the first issue of *Playboy* magazine, published in 1953?
A. $.30   B. $.50   C. $1.00

13. During the reign of Pope Pius V in early sixteenth-century Europe, prostitutes were called—
A. nuns   B. sisters of venery   C. she-devils

14. What were Gregory Pincus and John Rock inventors of?
A. tampons
B. silicone breast implants
C. oral contraceptives

15. Donatian Alphonse Francois was more familiarly known as—
A. Casanova
B. Marquis de Sade
C. Rudolph Valentino

16. King Louis XV of France helped populate the settlement of New Orleans by—
    A. holding a lottery for single marriageable females
    B. paying 3,000 francs to each female who sailed to America
    C. sending all of the prostitutes and criminals interned at La Saltpetriere Women's Prison

17. What do engaged couples in the rural Philippines sometimes exchange?
    A. locks of hair
    B. soiled clothes
    C. ornately carved mirrors to be hung in the boudoir on their wedding night

18. Worldwide, the most common form of marriage is—
    A. polygyny (a male with multiple wives)
    B. monogamy
    C. polyandry (a female with multiple husbands)

19. Which country has a culture that has no word for adultery in its vocabulary, and where the practice is socially acceptable?
    A. Brazil　B. New Guinea　C. India

20. Which country has an extremely sexually repressive society where the sexes are segregated throughout their lives, and intercourse, when it rarely occurs, is brief, perfunctory, and for the sole purpose of procreation?
    A. Ireland　B. Greenland　C. France

21. People of the Amazonian Mundurucu' tribe refer to intercourse as—
    A. "eating penises"
    B. "churning the cream"
    C. "fertilizing the crops"

22. Poachers are paid handsomely by Chinese black marketeers for what item?
    A. rhinoceros horn

    B. black bear gallbladders
    C. buffalo testicles

23. Who was the first president to be born in a hospital?
    A. Millard Fillmore
    B. Franklin Delano Roosevelt
    C. Jimmy Carter

24. An Arab husband who is absent from home for long periods may require his wife to protect her honor and fidelity by—
    A. locking her in the house and giving the key to his mother
    B. hiring a live-in chaperon to police her virtue
    C. infibulating (fastening) her genitals

25. A phylogynist is—
    A. a therapist that specializes in the treatment of female sexual psychosocial disorders
    B. a person that loves women
    C. a person that has a fetish for women's undergarments

26. An Englishman accused of "knicker picking" has done what?
    A. stolen women's panties
    B. pinched a female's buttocks
    C. had sex with an underage female

27. Siamese twins Chang and Eng Bunker, born joined at the chest in 1843, married the Yates sisters of North Carolina and fathered how many children?
    A. none   B. 2   C. 22

28. Which state has the highest birth rate?
    A. Alaska   B. California   C. Utah

29. What year did condom commercials first appear on television?
    A. 1984   B. 1987   C. 1990

30. What percent of U.S. babies are born to single or unmarried mothers?
    A. 15 percent   B. 19 percent   C. 25 percent

31. What percent of U.S. babies are born by cesarean section?
    A. 10 percent   B. 25 percent   C. 35 percent

32. Globally, what is the most prevalent mode of transmission of the AIDS virus?
    A. heterosexual intercourse
    B. intravenous drug use
    C. homosexual anal intercourse

33. Which country legally permits homosexual or same-sex marriages?
    A. Denmark   B. Sweden   C. Madagascar

34. Which country has 60 percent of AIDS cases worldwide?
    A. the United States   B. Africa   C. India

35. Before divorcing, American couples were typically married—
    A. 3 years   B. 7 years   C. 10 years

36. Who were the 1960s "Plaster Casters"?
    A. Moral vigilantes who vandalized adult bookstores by throwing bibles encased in plaster through the windows
    B. plaster reliefs made by naked participants of a "love-in"
    C. rock groupies who cast their idols' penises in plaster.

SEX . . . BODY BANTER!

Amazing Biological Facts

Human reproduction seems quite a miraculous phenomenon, since in order for fertilization to occur, hundreds of millions of sperm must travel over a quarter mile through microscopically tiny vessels (seminiferous tubules), endure a hostile acidic environment (vagina), and swim fast enough to be one of the several hundred lucky survivors to reach the fallopian tubes where conception takes place. A sperm's odds of fertilizing an egg are only slightly better than your chance of winning the state lottery jackpot. If that sperm carried a male-producing X chromosome the odds for successful implantation and pregnancy are further reduced. Biologically speaking, human males are definitely the weaker sex. The ratio of male to female conceptions is about 160:100 but because of the frailty of the male embryo, the actual live birth ratio is 105:100. While American women's reproductive years continue to increase each decade with earlier menarche (first menstruation) and later menopause, the sperm production and fertility of American men has, since the 1950s, decreased. Couples attempting to conceive, average five and one-half months of unprotected intercourse before succeeding. It's no wonder that humans engage in more copulations per conception than any primate.

1. The origin of the word "penis" is Latin, meaning "tail."

2. The flaccid penis varies between 8.5 cm. and 10.5 cm. in length, with an average of 9.5 cm., or approximately four inches.

3. From its flaccid state, the fully erect penis increases in length by an average of 7.5 cm., or roughly three inches.

4. When sexually stimulated, males under the age of forty are capable of achieving an erection in less than ten seconds.

5. The length of the average erect penis is approximately 12.5 cm. to 17.5 cm., or between five and seven inches.

6. A small flaccid penis generally has a greater percentage of increase to its erect size than a large flaccid penis.

7. The average circumference of the erect penis is 9.5 cm. or four inches.

8. The "Penile Plethysmograph," an electronic device capable of measuring minute changes in the circumference of the penis, is used for scientific research of male sexual arousal, treatment of chronic sex offenders, and studies on the effects of alcohol and sexual functioning.

9. The glans of the penis comprises 25 percent of its length.

10. Though genetically different, normal male and female fetuses are anatomically identical until the eighth week of gestation. By the twelfth week all internal and external sexual organs are fully formed.

11. "Dominican Republic syndrome," a rare inherited disorder, was discovered in the mid-1970s in rural Dominican Republic. Thirty-eight cases were documented of individuals born anatomically female, who, at puberty developed male genitalia and masculine sex characteristics. The Spanish term for this phenomenon is *guevodoces*, meaning "penis at twelve."

12. Male genitalia reach adult proportions at approximately 14.9 years of age.

13. Ultrasound tests have revealed that male fetuses have the capability for erections in the last trimester of gestation.

14. A male experiences an average of four to five erections nightly during the REM stage of sleep, occurring about every ninety minutes. There is no known relationship to sexual activity or frequency of intercourse and these cyclical nighttime erections.

15. Research has discovered that women also experience periodic nocturnal genital arousal similar to the pattern of men during REM sleep.

16. "Peyronie's disease" is a condition which causes the shaft of the penis to become permanently bent at an angle, making intercourse difficult and painful.

17. "Priapism," a male medical condition characterized by a spontaneous, prolonged, and often painful penile erection, is usually unrelated to sexual stimuli. Its name comes from Priapus, the Greek god of fertility, who, it was believed, possessed an abnormally large and perpetually erect penis. Incidentally, the treatment for this condition consists of "bleeding" the engorged penis by making small incisions along the base of the afflicted member.

18. "Micropenis" is a rare medical disorder that is characterized by an abnormally small penis measuring less than 2 cm., or 3/4 inch.

19. The left testicle usually hangs lower than the right, although the reverse may be true of left-handed men.

20. Approximately 50 percent of women have one breast that is larger than the other.

21. In cold weather, the muscles of the scrotum will contract, moving the testes closer to the body for warmth, and in warm weather will move them away from the body to keep them cooler.

22. During the excitement phase of sexual responsiveness, the testes will increase approximately 50 percent of their unstimulated size.

23. The seminiferous tubules which produce sperm in the testes, are tightly coiled microscopic vessels, that if laid out in a straight line, would extend to about five-hundred meters, or over a quarter mile in length.

24. From the onset of puberty, the mature male will produce billions of sperm annually.

25. Scientists have recently discovered that an essential protein of sperm which enables it to bind to the egg, is molecularly similar to snake venom.

26. Sperm production takes approximately seventy days.

27. Sperm is best produced at a bodily temperature three to four degrees lower than the normal 98.6 degrees Fahrenheit; that's why it is recommended that men wishing to conceive wear loose clothing and boxer shorts instead of tight restrictive clothing.

28. The uncontained penis is capable of ejaculating semen a distance of twelve to twenty-four inches.

29. The origin of the word "ejaculate" is from the Latin word *ejaculari*, meaning to "throw or shoot out."

30. The average ejaculation will produce approximately 5 ml. of semen—about one teaspoon.

31. In his lifetime a male will ejaculate approximately eighteen quarts of semen containing ½ trillion sperm.

32. There are approximately five calories in a teaspoon of semen.

33. Approximately one-hundred calories are burned during intercourse.

34. Over 600 million sperm may be present with one ejaculation of semen.

35. The average male's semen contains 10 percent abnormal sperm.

36. Most men are at peak fertility and produce the greatest amount of sperm between the ages of twenty to thirty.

37. Research has revealed that the sperm count of American men has declined since the 1950s.

38. Enough sperm to form an object slightly larger than an aspirin tablet would be sufficient to give Earth its present population.

39. The number of female ova to accomplish the same task would fill a large chicken egg.

40. A sperm cell measures a microscopic 1/500 of an inch.

41. Sperm can travel at an average speed of 1/8 inch per minute. It takes at least five minutes or longer to reach the site of fertilization in the fallopian tube.

42. From the moment of ejaculation within the vagina until migration to the site of fertilization in the fallopian tube, only about 300 of the original 200 to 400 million sperm will survive the journey.

43. After being ejaculated, sperm typically survive about forty-eight hours within the female body, but are capable of living as long as eight days.

44. It requires at least 20 million sperm per milliliter of semen for fertilization of an ovum to occur. Although only one sperm will fertilize an egg, it needs the assistance of hundreds of its fellow sperm to secrete hyaluronidase, an enzyme that breaks down the tough protective shell of the ovum.

45. An oral contraceptive for men is reportedly available in China. Developed from cottonseed oil, its active ingredient gossypol is thought to be an effective metabolic spermicide.

46. Male infertility is defined as the consistent ejaculation of fewer than 60 million sperm, of which less than 40 percent have motility.

47. Couples attempting to conceive average five and one-half months of unprotected intercourse before succeeding.

48. At midterm gestation, the ovaries of the female fetus contain approximately 6 to 7 million ova, or eggs, most of which will degenerate before birth.

49. At birth, the two ovaries contain 400,000 ova. Unlike a male's continual production of sperm, a female will form no additional ova.

50. Of the 400,000 immature eggs present at birth, only 400 will be ovulated successfully during a female's reproductive years— the rest will degenerate.

51. Some ova, or eggs, may lie dormant within the ovary for over forty years before reaching maturity in the ovulatory cycle.

52. The female egg measures 1/175 of an inch and is visible to the naked eye, appearing slightly smaller than the period at the end of this sentence. In fact, it's the largest cell in the human body.

53. An ovum is approximately 2,000 times larger than a sperm cell.

54. After being ovulated, the female egg will remain fertile for about twenty-four to forty-eight hours.

55. Although uncommon, it is possible for a woman to become pregnant during menses. While sperm generally survive about forty-eight hours in the female body, there have been documented cases of live sperm discovered eight days after intercourse.

56. During a normal pregnancy, the uterus will increase in weight from two ounces to over two pounds.

57. One female in one-thousand is born without a uterus.

58. In the United States, the average age of menarche, or onset

of first menstruation, is 12.8 years and continues to decrease each decade. One-hundred years ago, the average age of menarche was at age sixteen or older. A 1962 study showed that the age of first menstruation has decreased by four months in every decade since 1830.

59. While the average age of menarche has decreased, the age for menopause of American women has increased. In the latter part of the nineteenth century women experienced the onset of menopause in their forties; today, the average age is about fifty.

60. Menses lasts approximately three to seven days.

61. The average menstrual flow consists of approximately 50 to 175 cc, or ¼ to ¾ cup of blood and tissue.

62. Research has shown that female roommates or cohabiters may have closely timed or synchronized menstrual cycles. The theory is that pheromones secreted during the menstrual cycle by one roommate will affect the cycle of the other.

63. Studies have also demonstrated that during the peak estrogen production of midcycle, women have a more acute sense of smell, and are especially sensitive to musky odors.

64. The function of pubic hair is to act as an "odor trap" for secretions released by the apocrine glands located in the pubic and armpit areas. Once the secretions are released, the hair traps the scent, enabling it to linger and act as an erotic stimulus to the opposite sex. Incidentally, women possess 75 percent more scent glands than men.

65. A substance found in male sweat is molecularly similar to essence of sandalwood.

66. Pregnancy can significantly alter or diminish the sense of smell, which lends credibility to the long-held belief that it creates strange food cravings or aversions. Studies have shown that the sense of smell may be two thousand times greater before pregnancy than during it.

67. Among male primates, man has the largest (and thickest) organ of copulation.

68. Except among some higher primates, humans are the only mammals who engage in face-to-face intercourse.

69. Humans engage in more copulations per conception than any other primate.

70. Coitus lasts an average of ten to twenty minutes.

71. During intercourse, the male thrusts an average of sixty to one-hundred-twenty times.

72. During the excitement phase of sexual response, approximately 50 percent to 75 percent of women and 25 percent of men will develop a "sex flush" or light reddened rash on the trunk and/or extremities, which will subside quickly after orgasm.

73. In their study of human sexual response, the laboratory research of Masters and Johnson included observation of over ten thousand episodes of sexual activity.

74. The origin of the word "orgasm" is from the ancient Greek *orgaein*, meaning "to swell," or "be excited or lustful."

75. An orgasm lasts approximately 3 to 10 seconds, and the orgasmic contractions of both men and women occur at intervals of 0.8 seconds.

76. During orgasm, the heart averages 140 beats per minute.

77. Women have much greater orgasmic capabilities than men, and may experience multiple orgasms during a single sexual encounter.

78. "Anorgasmy" is the clinical term for the inability to have an orgasm. Recent studies indicate that approximately 10 percent of adult women have never experienced an orgasm.

79. Separate studies by the Kinsey Institute and Masters and

Johnson indicate that one percent of their female test subjects were able to achieve orgasm solely from breast stimulation.

80. The Association of Sex Educators, Counselors, and Therapists sponsored the three-day "International Conference on Orgasm," February 3, 1991, in New Delhi, India.

81. Testosterone, a hormone most commonly associated with "maleness," is produced in lesser quantities by females and is responsible for the sexual desire of both sexes.

82. Elevated testosterone levels in women, whether occurring naturally or artificially created by injection, will increase the female orgasmic response, the size of the clitoris, and may result in the growth of excess facial and body hair and deeper voice.

83. A study in 1975 revealed that men are more sexually attracted to women with enlarged pupils, a distinct pupillary response to their presence that demonstrates nonverbal sexual receptiveness on the part of the female.

84. "Passion purpura" is the medical term for a hickey.

85. The clinical term for hairy buttocks is "Daysypgal."

86. The pH of the vagina is 4.0 to 5.0—fairly acidic.

87. Female-producing sperm bearing a Y chromosome survive best in an acidic environment, while male-producing sperm with an X chromosome prefer an alkaline one.

88. The pleasurable highs associated with love are attributed to the brain's release of phenylethylamine, or PEA, a natural mood-altering substance that is also found in chocolate.

89. More than four ounces of alcohol will inhibit sexual arousal and performance.

90. There is no scientific evidence to support the long-held belief that saltpeter (potassium nitrate) will decrease male sexual desire or cause impotence.

91. More male fetuses are spontaneously aborted during pregnancy than females. Although the ratio of males to females at conception is 160:100—at birth it is 105:100.

92. According to Dr. David R. Reuben, author of *Everything You Always Wanted to Know About Sex But Were Afraid to Ask*, frequent intercourse in middle age may provide protection against the degenerative effects of arthritis. Intercourse stimulates the adrenal glands to produce cortisone, which alleviates symptoms of the disease.

93. "Bride's nose," or "Honeymoon catarrh," a condition which occurs during sexual arousal, is characterized by sneezing and a stuffy or running nose.

94. If you witness an act of "osculation," you are watching two people kiss.

95. It is possible for men to have an erection at the time of death.

SEX . . . THE WAY IT WAS!

Fascinating Historical Facts

While researching historical sexual data, it became evident that a significant pivotal event had the greatest impact on the sexual climate that followed. Sexual history witnessed a dramatic shift from the celebration of fertility and phallic worship by early Western civilizations, to the extreme denial and suppression of sexuality in later eras.

Little is known about the sex life of primitive man—only that he must have had one. The lack of prehistoric data from that early period is in sharp contrast to the historical largess passed on after the birth of Western civilization. Though great portions of ancient Greek and Roman cultural treasures (literature as well as art) were lost during the fall of the Roman Empire and the subsequent sacking of the Imperial city by invading Germanic hordes; that which could be salvaged found safe haven in the church. Thus began a peculiar relationship between the early Christians, curators and chroniclers of the historical remnants of a society they morally condemned, and the Romans, whose sexual excesses have never since been equaled. The moral condemnation of Roman licentiousness by the church and the sexually restrictive period which followed was a pattern that was to repeat itself throughout history with an ever-changing moral and sexual climate. And while the clergy was by and large responsible for shaping the prevailing sexual attitudes, they were disinclined to follow their own proscriptions. Ample anecdotal evidence through the ages revealed the sexual dichotomy that existed within the church; a dichotomy it could never reconcile

16

itself with, even to this day. The prohibition of sexual expression and carnality, even for married couples, was a directive of a church hierarchy rife with the very sexual excesses it sought to suppress. While the political climate of early European society had some influence on the existing moral attitudes, it was the pervasive doctrine of the church that was to shape the sexual mores of later Western civilization.

1. Shunammitism was an ancient religion that worshipped the healing powers of the scent and breath of the young virgins of Shunam.

2. The ceremonial rites of worship of the phallic god, Baalpeor, by the Moabites and Midianites, required circumcision of men, and the deflowering of young women by an artificial phallus.

3. It was the religious duty of Babylonian women to prostitute themselves at the temple in homage to the goddess Ishtar, who, it was believed, had chosen a particular male lover for the divine union. It was claimed by the Greek historian Herodotus that unattractive females might wait three or four years before being chosen. Not only were there female temple prostitutes, but male homosexual temple prostitutes as well.

4. First-born daughters of some Hindu sects were pledged to the temple at puberty to serve as religious sexual partners, and were thought to be the incarnation of the goddess Deva Desis. Barren women would also offer their services at the temple in hope of becoming fertile. Temple sex was regarded as a strictly religious experience, and no carnal pleasure was supposed to be derived from it.

5. It was the custom of some Romans to require the ritual deflowering of a virgin with the wooden phallus of the fertility god, Mutunus Tutunus, before consummation of her marriage.

6. A similar ceremony was practiced by the Hindu Lingyats. Young girls who pledged themselves to the moon god would be

deflowered by the lingham (phallus) of that god. Sterile women would also copulate with the lingham or offer sexual services at the temple to facilitate fertility.

7. In 1955, archaeologists in Corsica discovered prehistoric phallic monuments six to ten feet high, dating from the Bronze Age.

8. In Dimapur, on the India-Burma border, thirty giant phallic symbols twenty feet high, and twenty equally large replicas of the vagina, were erected in the fifteenth century by the Kacharis tribe.

9. During the festival honoring the goddess Ishtar, Babylonians prepared and ate breads and pastries shaped into replicas of male and female genitals.

10. *Phallophoriai* were phallic processions of ancient Greece which preceded specific fertility festivals such as the worship of Dionysus. Giant carved phalluses were carried aloft by phallopheroi, or "phallus bearers."

11. So sacred was the symbol of fertility and procreation that the early Hebrew tribes swore an oath on the phallus, much like our present custom of swearing on the bible.

12. The word "testes" originated from the Latin term *testiculus*, which denoted the ancient practice of placing a hand over the genitals, similar to today's practice of placing a hand over the heart, when swearing an oath.

13. Ancient cultures often wore phallic amulets and jewelry for good luck and fertility. An amulet known to historians as the "hand phallus" is today considered an obscene gesture. The artifact displays an extended middle finger, representing the erect penis, with the thumb folded over the other fingers.

14. Gesticulation with the extended middle finger was known by Romans as *digitus impudicus*, or "finger without shame."

15. The early Egyptians used hand signals as a form of sexual language, with different positions of the fingers used as symbols for male and female genitalia, intercourse, and other sexual acts.

16. The letter V, formed by displaying the index and middle finger, is recognized in Western culture as the victory sign, and briefly in the 1960s, as the "peace" sign. Of European origin, it was once used as an obscene gesture to suggest infidelity, and symbolized a double phallus. When displayed in the presence of the cuckolded husband, it meant, "Your wife has been cheating on you."

17. The swastika, synonymous with the Nazi movement, was said to have at one time been used to distinguish gender. If the tails of the cross pointed to the right it signified the male sex, pointing left, female.

18. The custom of placing an affectionate symbolic kiss in the form of an X following one's signature on a letter originated from the medieval practice of a largely uneducated and illiterate European society. An important document was usually signed with an X, which was then kissed as a display of sincerity.

19. From the thirteenth to fifteenth centuries the word "girl" was not a term that denoted gender, but referred to a young child of either sex.

20. Before the thirteenth century the word "husband" (from *hus* "house" and *bunda* "owner") simply meant any male who owned a house. Only wealthy feudal landowners owned houses, leasing small cottages on their estates to indentured serfs. A working man who was a homeowner was considered a prized marital prospect—most women desired a "husband" to wed.

21. Roman females were always given a feminized version of a male name such as Antonia, Theodora, or Agrippina. There were no exclusively female names in ancient Rome.

22. Archeological discoveries of the Mesopotamian region in-

dicate that female harems (from the Arabic *harim*, meaning "forbidden") existed as early as 3,000 B.C. During the seventh and eighth centuries A.D. the number of inhabitants of royal Persian households, such as those belonging to Caliphs Walid I, Abbasid, and Muqtadir, swelled to as many as four thousand persons.

23. The word "eunuch" is of Greek origin—*eune*, "bed" and *ekhein*, "to keep," and was a term for castrated males who were entrusted to guard the harems of nobility.

24. It is a common misconception that eunuchs were always impotent and incapable of performing sexually. Castration which consisted of removal of only the testes may have rendered the male sterile, but did not always impair the process of erection. It is claimed that eunuchs were often sought-after sexual partners because of their capability for prolonged erections.

25. The *castrati* of Italy were illustrious male sopranos who had been "sopranized," or castrated at a young age in order to preserve their high-pitched voices. Composer Joseph Hayden, who as a young boy sang in a choir at St. Stephen's Cathedral, was said to have narrowly escaped such a fate.

26. Only eunuchs were employed in the palace of Imperial China. It was such a prestigious position that young men from the provinces would apply for the job bearing their genitals in a jar.

27. At the age of thirty-three, Aurore Dudevant, better known as author George Sand, began an affair with twenty-seven-year-old composer Chopin that was to last for ten years.

28. Belladonna, meaning "fair lady," originated from the practice of Italian Renaissance women who customarily placed tincture of belladonna in their eyes. Used cosmetically, it darkened and enlarged the pupil, making the eye more attractive, as well as enhancing the pale complexion which was fashionable during that age.

29. Men of the Middle Ages sometimes wore a *poulaine*; a long phallic-shaped shoe.

30. During the Tudor period (1550), men wore a *braquette* or codpiece which simulated an erection and caused a conspicuous bulge in the trousers. It is claimed that the largest codpiece on display at the Tower of London belonged to King Henry VIII.

31. Young men of ancient Greece had no immodesty about openly or publicly displaying their genitals. The word "gymnastics" comes from the Greek *gymnos*, meaning "naked." Participants of games and competitive sports were usually unclothed.

32. When exercising nude at the gymnasium, young Greek men would often tie the foreskin over the glans of the penis to prevent injury. This practice was known in Greek as *kynodesme*, or "dog tie."

33. The practice of circumcision can be traced back to ancient Egypt, and was performed as a hygienic ritual. While the Egyptians considered the uncircumcised male to be a coarse barbarian, the fifth-century Greeks held a similar impression of the circumcised male.

34. It was estimated that in the 1950s approximately 85 percent of male babies born in the United States were circumcised.

35. Ancient Greeks admired the small firm penis, and considered the large member aesthetically unappealing.

36. Aristotle proposed that a small penis was capable of greater fertility than a large one because the sperm had less distance to travel, therefore it was more "hot and potent."

37. Aristotle also believed that conception resulted from semen combining with menstrual blood, and that a woman's most fertile time was during menses.

38. The term menses originated from the latin word *mensis*, meaning "month," or from the Greek *mene*, for "moon."

39. Tertullian, a Christian polemist, believed that the formation of a person happened at the moment of ejaculation, and that the act of fellatio, in which semen was swallowed, was an act of cannibalism.

40. It was a popular belief during the Middle Ages that both men and women produced sperm.

41. Antonie van Leeuwenhoek, an optician from Delft, first discovered and named spermatozoa. The scientifically advanced Royal Society of London published his findings in 1678.

42. In the early 1800s it was commonly believed that the female ovum was released during the act of intercourse.

43. During the Middle Ages menstruating women were not allowed into the church or permitted to handle meat or certain foods. It was believed that edibles touched by women during menses would become contaminated or soiled. This prohibition persists today in some preliterate societies.

44. Victorian-era women were expected to be incapacitated by menstruation, and often retreated to their "sick beds" to be treated like frail invalids.

45. The first disposable sanitary napkin (called a "sanitary towel" by the British) was marketed in the late 1800s, but did not become widely popular until after World War I when Kimberly-Clark introduced its product "Kotex." Made from cellulose rather than cotton, it was originally developed as a surgical compress, and because of its superior absorbency, quickly gained favor among nurses, who used it as a menstrual pad.

46. On September 12, 1933, Denver gynecologist Dr. Earle Cleveland Haas obtained a patent for the internally-worn tampon. He created his registered trademark "Tampax" from the words "tampon" and "vaginal pack."

47. Ancient Egyptian women fashioned tampons from rolls of

softened papyrus; the Japanese used paper, and Roman matrons, wads of wool.

48. Women of ancient Rome and Greece practiced depilation, or removal of their pubic hair.

49. An adulterous Greek male was sometimes punished by the removal of his pubic hair and the insertion of a large radish into his rectum.

50. The Roman punishment for adultery was often amputation of the nose.

51. In A.D. 870, the nuns of a convent in Coldingham, Scotland, slashed off their noses and upper lips to successfully repel their would-be Scandinavian rapists.

52. English monarch King Canute (or Cnut) (1017–1030) decreed that a wife found guilty of adultery must have her ears and nose cut off—a punishment that King Louis XIV of France (1643–1713) favored for discouraging prostitution.

53. During the Dark Ages if a woman was suspected of adultery, a heavy stone was tied around her neck and she was thrown into a large body of water. If she managed to float, she was proven innocent.

54. An offender found guilty of bestiality in the Middle Ages was burned at the stake, along with the animal involved in the alleged incident.

55. Puritan women prosecuted for adultery in Plymouth, Massachusetts, were subject to a law which stated that the offender must be publicly flogged and required to wear a large scarlet letter **A** on her breast for the rest of her life.

56. During the Gold Rush of the 1800s it was a prevailing superstition that if the flame of a miner's candle extinguished three times it was an omen that his wife was committing adultery or being raped.

57. After discovering his wife Catherine in an adulterous affair, Russian czar Peter I forced her to watch her lover's execution, then had the unfortunate man's head pickled in spirits and placed in her bedroom. It is also claimed that Peter I had likewise rendered the head of his unfaithful mistress, a Mrs. Hamilton, and kept her preserved head in *his* bedchamber.

58. The 1625 settlement of Merry Mount, in Plymouth, Massachusetts, founded by Thomas Morton, became notorious among the colonies for its acceptance of extramarital sex among its inhabitants, as well as condoning sexual relations between settlers and the local Indian population. Morton was also responsible for reestablishing the pagan May Day rites, during which the phallic Maypole was erected.

59. In the mid-1800s, John Humphrey Noyes founded a utopian group in Oneida, New York, the "Perfectionists," who practiced a form of communal group marriage and child-rearing. All members were sexually available to one another for heterosexual relations, though sex partners and couples desiring to have children were selected by a committee. Adolescent males were taught sexual techniques, especially *coitus reservatus* (the ability to prolong an erection and delay ejaculation), by older menopausal women.

60. Until 1884, an English Victorian-era woman could be imprisoned for denying her husband his conjugal rights.

61. "Flourish" was the polite Victorian euphemism for intercourse.

62. The primary role of the early Greek wife was to provide her husband with legitimate male heirs, leaving her sexual needs often disregarded. Wives were frequently addressed as "woman," or *gyne*, which literally meant "childbearer." Men usually sought sexual gratification from slaves, prostitutes, concubines, or young boys. To impart some fairness to the situation the Athenian legislator Solon (sixth century B.C.), decreed that a

husband was obliged to have intercourse with his wife at least three times a month.

63. Solon was also responsible for a law which allowed fathers to sell their unvirtuous daughters into slavery.

64. Ancient Babylonian law allowed husbands to offer their wives as collateral to obtain a loan. If the debt went unpaid, the wife, along with other household goods, was confiscated.

65. The *gynaikonomoi*, or "women's police," was a special female law enforcement division in Athens whose responsibility was to restrict the movement and ensure the virtue of respectable Greek women.

66. The Roman poet Ovid suggested in his writings that the ultimate sexual experience came from the pursuit and conquest of another man's wife, with a long and arduous seduction yielding the greatest amount of pleasure.

67. The fifth century *Kama Sutra*, meaning "love precepts," written by Mallanga Vatsyayana, is a Hindu instructional book of sexual techniques which describes ten types of kisses, sixty-four different caresses and acts of foreplay, eight variations of oral-genital stimulation, and eighty-four positions for intercourse. It is claimed that Vatsyayana had no practical experience of the subject and was a Hindu aesthetic who lived a celibate life, creating his sexual treatise through "divine knowledge."

68. Romans had three different terms for the act of kissing, which distinguished between an acquaintance (*basium*), a close friend or relative (*osculum*), and a lover (*suavium*).

69. The "French kiss" was first known as *maraichinage*, a term to describe the prolonged, deep, tongue kiss practiced by the Maraichins, inhabitants of Brittany, France.

70. The Greek word for pig, *choiros*, was also used as ancient descriptive slang for vagina (i.e., cunt).

71. It was considered improper for Romans to have intercourse before nightfall, in a lighted room, or for Roman women to fully disrobe for sex. Only fallen women would allow their breasts to be exposed. Fifth-century Greek women also adhered to these prohibitions.

72. Women in ancient Rome gave birth while seated in a specially designed birthing chair.

73. Wealthy Roman men would often keep a preferred child slave for sexual purposes.

74. In ancient Greece and Rome, homosexuality was an acknowledged and accepted practice of society, even among those with traditional heterosexual marriages.

75. The frequent depiction of rear-entry sexual positions on Greek pottery, suggestive of anal intercourse, indicates that it was a preferred homosexual, as well as heterosexual practice.

76. In late nineteenth-century Germany, homosexuals were called "urnings," probably in reference to homosexual acts depicted on ancient Greek and Roman urns.

77. The pederastic homosexual acts that Greek men performed with young boys included not only anal intercourse, but frequently intercrural copulation (between the thighs).

78. Although the island of Lesbos is synonymous with lesbianism, the ancient Greeks associated it with the practice of fellatio. The Greek verbs *lesbiazo* and *lesbizo* refer to the act of fellatio.

79. The fifth-century Greek and Roman *symposium* was primarily a male social function where guests engaged in feasting and drinking, were entertained by dancers, musicians, and sexual performances, and often participated in group sex with prostitutes, slaves, or young boys. The *symposium* is primarily responsible for the legend of the "Roman orgy."

80. *Olisboi*, meaning "to glide or slip," were ancient dildos made of leather, and were sometimes used in sexual performances or exhibitions.

81. It is claimed that Theodora, the wife of Byzantine emperor Justinian (527–565 B.C.), performed as a striptease dancer and entertained thousands of spectators with the shocking display of geese pecking grain from her genitals.

82. While Roman emperor Claudius was engaged in a military campaign in Britain, his young wife Valeria Messalina caused a scandal by turning a palace bedroom into a brothel and servicing the male public for the standard legal fee. Her nymphomania was legend, and it is claimed that she once challenged the most popular and well-known prostitute in Rome to a contest—the winner to be determined by the most copulations within twenty-four hours. Pliny the Elder declared Messalina the winner, having beaten her rival by twenty-five men.

83. Napoleon Bonaparte's sister, Pauline, suffered from periodic bouts of nymphomania, and was said to favor lovers with large members. She became physically exhausted and suffered from "vaginal distress" after engaging in a yearlong affair with the overly endowed Nicholas Philippe Auguste de Forbin, an Italian painter. With her health at risk, she was finally persuaded by her personal physician to end the relationship.

84. It's claimed that the first publicized nude performance of our era occurred at the Paris *Folies Bergese* in 1912.

85. H. L. Mencken befriended stripper Gypsie Rose Lee (1914–1970) and coined the term "ecdysiast" (from the Greek "getting out" and "molting"), to lend respectability to the art of stripteasing.

86. It was the custom in ancient Greece and Rome to bathe in nude communal bathhouses; a practice that remained popular throughout medieval Europe, and which later became associated

with commercial vice. It is from this link to prostitution that early European bordellos were referred to as "stews."

87. On Labor Day 1929, Kurt Barthel founded the first organization in the United States devoted to nudism. Later that year, a meeting in a gymnasium of "The American League for Physical Culture" was raided by police.

88. The first issue of *Playboy* magazine appeared in December 1953, and sold for $.50. Its centerfold was a nude calendar photo of Marilyn Monroe purchased by Hugh Hefner for $500.

89. It's claimed that before he became the successful publisher of *Playboy* magazine, Hugh Hefner was, at one time during his career, employed by *Children's Activities* magazine.

90. The April 1972 issue of *Cosmopolitan* featured actor Burt Reynolds as the first nude male centerfold of a popularly read magazine.

91. Designer Rudi Gernreich gained brief notoriety in 1964 when he introduced a topless swimsuit to the American public. Several women wearing this daring new design were arrested for indecent exposure.

92. The marriageable age for young Roman girls was at puberty, and it was not uncommon for girls as young as twelve to wed. A person of fourteen was considered an adult.

93. June—named for the goddess Juno, guardian of women and marriage—has been the favorite month for weddings since ancient Roman times.

94. In 1875 the legal age of consent for a British female was raised to thirteen.

95. Wearing a wedding ring on the third finger of the left hand may have originated from the belief of ancient Egyptians and Greeks that the primary vein of that finger (*vena amoris*, "love vein") traveled directly to the heart

96. The custom of a white wedding gown did not become popular until the nineteenth century. Prior to that time, brides favored black or gray dresses that wouldn't soil easily and could be worn for other social occasions such as baptisms and funerals.

97. Ancient Roman brides covered their heads with a *flameum*, or red veil, to symbolize the "flames of passion."

98. The ancient Islamic law of Muhammadan allowed a "*mut'a* marriage"; a contractual union that was to last for a specified length of time, or a type of trial marriage.

99. Herodotus, a fifth-century B.C. Greek historian and story-teller, claimed that the marriage customs of the Nasamones of Libya required the bride to sleep with all of the male celebrants at the wedding party.

100. Indian Caribs were reported to celebrate the wedding of a *cacique* (chief), by offering the bride to all other *caciques* invited to the festivities.

101. During the Dark Ages feudal lords exercised *le droit du seignur*, "the right of the lord," or *jus primae noctis*, "right of the first night," which allowed them to deflower a new bride before consummation of her marriage.

102. Medieval English wedding celebrations were usually drunken, raucous affairs where great quantities of ale were consumed. During the eleventh century, a feast honoring the bride was called "bride ale," which later evolved into the word we now recognize as "bridal."

103. Egyptian Pharaoh Rameses II was said to have fathered 160 children.

104. Incan and Egyptian royalty permitted incestuous marriages between siblings to ensure a lineage of pure royal blood. In some ancient cultures it was compulsory for an heir to the throne to marry his sister. The Ptolemies, a Greek dynasty, were said to have practiced marriage between siblings for over three hundred

years with no physical or mental defects of offspring. Cleopatra was the sixth generation to be born of such a union.

105. Before her notorious affairs with Julius Caesar and Marc Antony, Cleopatra was wed in succession to two of her brothers, Ptolemy XII and Ptolemy XIII.

106. Julia Agrippina engaged in an incestuous relationship with her brother, Roman emperor Caligula, and later married her uncle, emperor Claudius. It is also rumored that she had been intimate with her son, the disreputable Nero.

107. The infamous Lucrezia Borgia was the illegitimate daughter of Borgia Rodrigo Lanzol, who later became Pope Alexander VI. It was claimed that she was involved in incestuous relationships with her father, and later, her brother.

108. Pope Alexander VI was the host of orgies attended by prostitutes. At one such event, fifty nude prostitutes serviced a group of men, with a prize awarded to the male partygoer who displayed the most stamina.

109. In the mid-1400s it was believed that incest upon the altar was an effective prophylactic against the plague.

110. A marriage custom of the fourteenth century required the newlywed couple to be escorted to the marital bed by family members and the priest, who offered a blessing prior to consummation of their union. The bloody bed sheet was displayed the morning after as proof of a successful sexual encounter.

111. The modern custom of throwing the bride's garter originated from the early European ritual of pulling off the newlywed couple's stockings by the bridal party and flinging them about the bedchamber. Lore has it that if a sock landed on either the new husband or wife; the person who threw it, if they were of the opposite sex, would be the next to marry.

112. The early Christian church required newlywed couples to abstain from sex for three nights after the wedding ceremony; a custom called "the Tobias nights." After the marriage was consummated, the couple could not enter the church for thirty days.

113. So sexually repressive was medieval Christian doctrine, that coitus was to be avoided whenever possible. Intercourse was solely for procreation, with no carnal pleasure derived from the act. The invention of the *chemise cagoule*, a stiff nightshirt with a strategically placed hole, ensured that intercourse could occur with no direct bodily contact between partners.

114. Cartharism, a religious movement of the Middle Ages, prohibited its adherents from engaging in marital sex, believing that abstinence facilitated spiritual enlightenment.

115. The Bulgarians, devout followers of Cartharism, had an extremely low birth rate and were consequently accused of practicing anal intercourse, a popular belief which spawned the term "buggery."

116. Sylvester Graham (1794–1851), inventor of the graham cracker, was a vegetarian who advocated sexual abstinence and promoted the belief that eating meat, condiments, and spices would arouse carnal desire and inflame one's libido. Graham suggested that it was better for one's health to limit intercourse to twelve times a year.

117. Cornflake baron John Harvey Kellogg was repulsed by sexual intercourse and never consummated his marriage in 1879 to Ella E. Eaton. He had the odd habit of receiving a daily enema after breakfast. Kellogg was the author of several treatises denouncing sexual excess and masturbation, which he believed caused physical debilitation and moral degeneracy. His book, *Plain Facts for Old and Young Embracing the Natural History and Hygiene of Organic Life*, which he wrote on his honeymoon, offers thirty-nine signs for detection of "the secret vice of self-

abuse.'' Some of the more interesting examples are shuffling or unsteady gait, round shoulders, unnatural paleness, eating clay, chalk or slate pencils, acne, mock piety, and general debility.

118. It's been claimed that St. Swithin, in order to prove his moral strength and resistance to carnal temptation, shared his bed with two beautiful young virgins.

119. St. Origen proclaimed that "women are the gates of hell," then proceeded to castrate himself.

120. It was reported that the infamous Pope John XII transformed the Church of St. John Lateran into a brothel. Following his excommunication from the church in A.D. 963, he suddenly died while engaged in an act of adultery.

121. Church-controlled brothels were not uncommon in medieval Europe. Queen Joanna, of Naples, established one of the first such brothels, named "abbaye" or abbey. Only Christians were allowed to patronize the house, and its female residents were required to observe the hours of prayer and regularly attend religious services. Church hierarchy such as priests, mother superiors, archbishops, and even Pope Julius II, were known to be involved in the operation of such establishments.

122. In early sixteenth-century Europe, during the reign of Pope Pius V, harlots and courtesans were referred to as "nuns" and a brothel, a "nunnery."

123. The cost of constructing St. Peter's Basilica, in Rome, was partially financed from a church-imposed prostitution tax originating from the Middle Ages—a fund that proved an even greater source of revenue than the sale of "indulgences" (payment to the church for redemption of sins).

124. Although there was a prohibition of priestly marriage within the Catholic church dating from the fifth century, the vow of celibacy wasn't strictly enforced until the 1920 decree of Pope Benedict XV.

125. During the witchcraft epidemic of the Middle Ages it was thought that the devil seduced and had intercourse with persons in the form of a devil-spirit called an *incubus* (male spirit), or *sucubus* (female spirit).

126. At the height of the witchcraft inquisitions in 1400, the Saxon civil courts made copulation with the devil a capital crime, punishable by hanging or burning to death at the stake.

127. Confessions obtained through various means of torture by the inquisitors revealed that intercourse with the devil was painful, due to his abnormally large organ, and that his semen was ice-cold.

128. The Greek legend of the fierce Amazon women warriors claims that as young girls they burned off their breasts, enabling them to better handle a bow and arrow, hence acquiring the name *amazone*, meaning "breastless."

129. The invention of the chastity belt, first known as "the Girdle of Venus" or "the Florentine Girdle," was said to originate from Homer's *Odyssey*, in which Aphrodite's husband, Hephaistos, forged a girdle as punishment for her marital infidelities.

130. The concept of Cupid originated from the Greek mythological figure Eros, son of Aphrodite, represented as a beautiful young boy who was considered the embodiment of sexual love. During the sexually repressive Victorian era, he was depicted wearing a skirt.

131. The Greek god Adonis was thought to be responsible for women having orgasms.

132. Syphilis obtained its name from a medical poem written during the Renaissance by Verona physician Girolamo Fracastoro, who revised the Greek legend of a shepherd named Syphilus who was stricken with a scourge as punishment for offending the sun god during a period of drought.

133. Sixteenth-century French physician Jacques de Bethencourt is responsible for the term "venereal disease," which originated from *morbus venerus*, "the sickness of Venus," goddess of love. He coined the term to describe diseases that occurred as a result of intercourse.

134. It was thought that syphilis was first introduced to Europe between 1494–1497 when Columbus's sailors returned to Portugal from Haiti; the disease spread quickly throughout the continent. During this same period a "genital pox" that swept rapidly through the ranks of the French army in Naples was named *morbus gallicus* or "French sickness." Aboard sailing vessels, outbreaks of venereal disease were often referred to as "lady's fever."

135. Mercury, a favorite nineteenth-century treatment for syphilis, often caused the user to have bad breath and purple gums. Its use sometimes resulted in death.

136. Another unconventional treatment for syphilis was exposing the patient to malaria in the belief that the high fever which resulted would provide a cure.

137. The term "gonorrhea," of Greek origin, meaning "flow of seed," was named by Galen (1300–200 A.D.) to describe the painful discharge of pus from the genitals.

138. While gonorrhea had been in existence as long as syphilis, it was mistaken for an early stage of the latter. Its discovery as a separate disease, by Dr. Philip Ricord, didn't occur until the mid-nineteenth century. Gonorrhea probably flourished unabated for centuries, because mercury, the treatment of the age for syphilis, was ineffective against the gonococcus.

139. In 1897 Albert Neisser, a twenty-four-year-old German medical researcher, was first to identify and name the organism which causes gonorrhea—the gonococcus.

140. *Spirochaeta pallida*, the organism responsible for causing

syphilis, was first identified by Russian zoologist Fritz Schaudinn, though not until the early twentieth century.

141. Syphilis was at one time known as *lues*.

142. The active sex life of Catherine the Great of Russia has been the subject of much rumor and speculation by historians. It's been said that during her reign she employed in her court six *les empreuves*, or "testers," female aides whose responsibility was to screen potential lovers for sexual prowess and venereal disease.

143. The "Wassermann," a blood test introduced in 1906 to diagnose the presence of syphilis, was named for its inventor, Berlin bacteriologist August von Wassermann.

144. Penicillin was introduced in 1944 as a treatment for venereal disease.

145. A controversial study of four hundred syphilis-infected black men in Macon County, Alabama, was conducted by the U.S. Public Health Service from 1932–1971 to research the long-range effects of the untreated disease. Although an effective cure (penicillin) had been developed during that time, treatment was withheld from the unsuspecting participants who believed they were receiving medical care. Survivors of the study, and the families of deceased participants, received a $9 million settlement from the U.S. government in 1974.

146. The precursor of the condom was a linen sheath designed in 1564 by anatomist Gabriello Fallopio, and worn as a protection from venereal disease. The fallopian tubes of the female reproductive system also bear his name.

147. Before the advent of rubber, condoms were constructed from animal cecums (small intestines). A seventeenth-century physician, Dr. Conton, is credited with producing the first such devices, fashioned from fish bladders and lambskin.

148. After the invention of vulcanized rubber (1843–49) by

Goodyear and Hancock, the condom, or "rubber" as it was
known, was first introduced at the Philadelphia World Exposition
in 1878. By 1930 more than 317 million condoms were being
sold annually.

149. The "French letter," a Victorian euphemism for a condom, was known by the French as *la capote anglaise*—"the
English cape."

150. A form of the contraceptive sponge was in use as early as
the 1800s. Before insertion it was first soaked in a solution of
quinine, used as a spermicide, and had a string attached for easy
removal.

151. The diaphragm was invented in 1842 by a German anatomy
professor, Dr. W.P.J. Mensinga.

152. "The Human Birth Control Appliance," patented on October 27, 1970, is a device that is worn like a panty, and contains
an expandable crotch which is pushed into the vagina during
intercourse, acting as a mechanical barrier to conception or venereal disease.

153. Anthony Comstock, the secretary of the New York Society
for the Suppression of Vice, was instrumental in the passage of
the Comstock Act of 1873, a federal law which prohibited the
distribution of birth control information through the mail. He was
responsible for the destruction of over 160 tons of contraceptive
literature which he called "lewd, lascivious, and obscene."

154. The Supreme Court did not overturn the laws prohibiting
distribution of birth control information until 1965.

155. Margaret Sanger, an early American feminist and social
reformer, is credited with the term "birth control," and in 1914
founded the Birth Control League, later renamed Planned Parent-
hood Federation of America.

156. The former Soviet government legalized abortion on No-

vember 18, 1920. Today, between 7 and 21 million women receive therapeutic abortions annually.

157. The first laws prohibiting abortion were enacted by the state of Connecticut in May 1821, although the abortion trade flourished unabated for the next century. American society deemed it morally acceptable to terminate a pregnancy if the mother had not yet experienced "quickening" of the fetus, believing there was no fetal life until internal movement could be felt.

158. Seventeenth-century abortionists openly advertised their services in popularly read newspapers and periodicals under the guise of treating "private disorders of the female," or offering help for "monthly blockage," and "female suppression." A mail-order pill business thrived during this period, dispensing "abortifacients," which were combinations of botanical extracts known to be strong purgatives, such as black cohosh, hemlock, ergot, and snakeroot.

159. The first legislation in the United States to legalize abortion was enacted April 25, 1967, by the state of Colorado. Governor John Arthur Love signed into law the right to obtain an abortion granted by approval of a three-doctor board of an accredited hospital.

160. In January 1973, Texas attorney Sarah Weddington successfully argued before the Supreme Court on behalf of "Jane Roe," resulting in the monumental decision that allowed American women the legal right to obtain an abortion.

161. In the mid-1900s some European countries were using X rays as a means of voluntary sterilization of women.

162. Before the advent of the vasectomy, male inmates of American mental institutions were often castrated. It's been reported that in 1906 the state of California made the practice compulsory. Masturbation was commonly believed to cause in-

sanity, and castration offered a possible cure for mental disorders caused by such sexual excesses.

163. Research scientists Gregory Pincus and John Rock were inventors of the first oral contraceptive, Envoid, introduced to the U.S. market in the late 1950s by the Searle Company.

164. Mallangia Vatsyayana, author of the *Kama sutra*, recommended eating the blossoms of the Palash flower as an effective means of contraception. Interestingly, medical research conducted on rats in the 1960s showed that this method of contraception was effective in 80 percent of the animals.

165. Contraceptive practices of 1950 B.C. Egyptians included the use of pessaries made of crocodile dung and honey, and vaginal fumigations of an ancient drug known as *minnis*.

166. To prevent conception, the Roman poet Lucretius advocated violent shaking of the body to expel semen after intercourse.

167. Pliny the Elder recommended wearing an amulet made of the worms of a hairy spider as a contraceptive.

168. Athenian women rubbed oil of cedar and ointment of lead on their cervix to prevent conception.

169. An ancient cervical cap was devised by sixth-century Greek physician Aetius, who recommended cutting a pomegranate in half, scooping out the flesh, then inserting it into the vagina prior to intercourse.

170. Chastity belts, worn by women during the Crusades, were devices made of leather and metal that when locked securely in place, allowed for the passage of human waste, but prevented the wearer from having intercourse with anyone other than the person holding the key.

171. As late as 1933, the League of Awakened Magyars advocated chastity belts for all unmarried girls over the age of twelve.

172. During the 1820s, Dr. Weinhold of Halle der Saale infibulated unmarried males as a method of contraception and also as a deterrent to masturbation. The procedure consisted of piercing the foreskin with a thin wire, then soldering the ends together. The infibulation was left intact until marriage.

173. Victorian English society considered masturbation a pathological perversion that should be prevented by any means possible. In 1908 a nurse designed and patented a cagelike device with spikes protruding from it, which fit over a young boy's genitals and was locked in place with a key.

174. In the 1800s, to prevent a nocturnal erection in a young boy, a metal ring with spikes on the inner surface was placed around the base of the penis. A nighttime erection would cause the wearer to awaken from sleep.

175. It is claimed that the practice of circumcising Western, non-Jewish males was not purely for hygienic purposes, but rather to prevent young males from indulging in masturbation. Its popularity in Western culture evolved from the Victorian sexual repression of the late nineteenth century. On the vanguard of this movement was British surgeon James Hunter, whose 1891 treatise *On Circumcision as Preventative of Masturbation* typified the mores of that era.

176. Treatment for female masturbation in the mid-1800s was often surgical removal of the clitoris.

177. The origin of the word masturbate is from the Latin *manu* (hand), and *stuprare* (to defile), and was at one time referred to as "Onanism," a term coined by Hume in his 1766 *Treatise Upon the Disorders Produced by Masturbation*. Hume based his writing on the Old Testament tale of God's punishment of Onan for "spilling his seed upon the ground"; a story, oddly, that referred to coitus interruptus (withdrawal of the penis from the vagina prior to ejaculation), rather than masturbation.

178. Swiss physician S. Tissot (1728–1797) was responsible for

promoting the belief that masturbation caused nerve damage and insanity by forcing blood to rush to the head.

179. Few people will recognize the name Donatien Alphonse Francois, Lord of La Coste and *Cosiegnuer* of Mazan—destined to be remembered throughout history as the Marquis de Sade.

180. The Marquis de Sade, born June 2, 1740, died in an insane asylum in 1814 at the age of seventy-four.

181. The term "masochism" originated after the publication of *Venus in Furs*, by author Leopold Baron von Sacher-Masoch (1836–1905), the first of many novels he wrote depicting sexual pleasure derived from female domination and the infliction of pain.

182. During sexually repressive periods such as the early Christian movement, and the Puritan and Victorian eras, flagellation was a common practice for sexual gratification. From the Dark Ages until the Renaissance, considered one of the most sexually restrictive periods, hysteria, insanity, and perversions were rampant.

183. Theresa Berkley, a London brothelkeeper, gained famed during the early nineteenth century as the "Queen of the Flagellants," and is credited with inventing the "Berkley Horse"—a mechanical device which could expertly flog her clients.

184. French author Marcel Proust (1871–1922) was a bisexual who was reported to have financed a sadomasochistic homosexual brothel in order to indulge his voyeuristic pleasure at watching patrons being whipped.

185. In 1897 Dr. Magnus Hirschfeld founded the Hirschfeld Institute for Sexuality in Charlottenburg, Germany, one of the first such institutions devoted to the study of human sexuality. A homosexual, he was responsible for the term "transvestism."

186. The word "homosexuality" was not used until 1809. Prior

to that time, it was referred to as "inversion," and homosexuals, as "inverts."

187. Dr. Alfred Kinsey officially established the nonprofit Institute for Sex Research in 1947.

188. Successful artificial insemination of a human female was accomplished in the 1780s by Scottish surgeon John Hunter. He also conducted unorthodox research of venereal disease, infecting himself with gonorrhea and syphilis by making small incisions on his penis then swabbing the cuts with a probe that had been dipped into the lesion of an infected prostitute. His efforts resulted in a syphilitic lesion bearing his name—the "hunterian chancre." He died with the mistaken belief that gonorrhea and syphilis were different stages of the same disease.

189. Gynecologist James Marion Simms (1813–1889), the first American physician to duplicate John Hunter's artificial insemination procedure, was also credited with the invention of the vaginal speculum, a device which revolutionized examination and treatment of gynecological disorders.

190. A mid-nineteenth century treatment for cervical and uterine inflammation included the application of eight to ten leeches via a speculum onto the external cervix, a procedure also thought to induce miscarriage of an unwanted pregnancy. Complications often arose when a leech would accidentally creep into the uterus.

191. The Pap smear was invented in 1935 by a U.S. pathologist, Dr. George N. Papanicolaou, to aid in the detection of cervical cancer.

192. Greek midwives treated postpartum bleeding by orally administering goat's urine and dung.

193. In the early Middle Ages it was thought that to arouse sexual desire in a man, the wife could coat her naked body with honey, roll in a pile of wheat, carefully remove the grains from the skin, then mill them counterclockwise. The bread dough

prepared from this flour was then carefully kneaded between the upper thighs (i.e., genitals). After consuming this bread, a man was supposed to have heightened libido and sexual prowess. To render a man impotent, the same procedure was followed, except the grain was milled clockwise.

194. Another method for increasing sexual desire of men in the Middle Ages involved placing a fish in the woman's vagina until it died, whereupon it was cooked and served to the husband.

195. An Italian Renaissance woman wishing to seduce a potential lover would feed him *confarreatio* cake, a confection thought to have magical qualities. The cake was put in a small oven which was placed over the naked pudendum and baked by the "heat of passion" the individual possessed for her intended amour.

196. The custom of serving wedding cake following the ceremony has its origin in the *confarreatio* cakes (small wheat cakes) eaten by the newlywed couple of ancient Rome to ensure fertility. This ritual was of such importance that the marriage ceremony was referred to as a *confarreation* (wheat-wedding or ceremony of eating wheat together).

197. A sixteenth-century test for female fertility consisted of inserting a clove of garlic in the vagina. If, after a period of twelve hours, the patient's breath emitted the odor of garlic, then fertility was assured.

198. The "Bitterling test" was a nineteenth-century pregnancy test using a Bitterling, a small carp-like fish found in Eastern European waters. When placed in a quart of water with two teaspoons of female urine, the prominent oviducts of the fish, stimulated by hormones, would descend if the woman was pregnant.

199. Many eighteenth-century French brothels contained *salles de preparations*, which were special rooms for the preparation of aphrodisiacs, lotions, and cosmetics.

200. The ancient Roman brothel was called a *lupanar*, or "she-wolves den."

201. A Roman prostitute was officially called *meretrix*, meaning "earner," or one who earns her living with her body.

202. It is said that in ancient Rome there were twelve ranks of prostitutes, from the affluent *delicatae*, or "kept women," to the destitute *quadrantariae* who would often provide sexual services for a piece of bread. The *bustuariae* were cemetery prostitutes who supplemented their income as paid mourners at funerals.

203. The word "fornication" (sex between unmarried persons), is derived from the Latin word *fornix*, meaning "archway." Roman street prostitutes found brisk trade underneath the arches of the Coliseum, servicing male patrons whose passions were aroused by the blood and violence of the games, or an erotically stimulating play.

204. Roman prostitutes who plied their wares in the streets were required by law to wear a short *tunica* and dye their hair yellow with saffron, to distinguish them from the dark-haired, more conservatively dressed patrician women of the city.

205. Roman whores often painted or gilded their breasts and nipples.

206. *Hetairai* ("lady friend" or "companion"), were the courtesans of ancient Greece and Rome, and were a class of women valued for their culture, education, and sexual expertise. The freedom and status they enjoyed in society was much greater than that of the Roman matron.

207. Solon, a sixth-century B.C. Athenian legislator, instituted the state-controlled brothel. Legalized brothels included male homosexual as well as heterosexual establishments, and fees for the various sexual services offered were regulated by the government.

208. In order to control its growing prostitution trade, the city of

New Orleans passed a law in 1897 that required all madams and prostitutes to be licensed and taxed.

209. The standard fee charged by the *meretrices*, Rome's legal prostitutes, was one *obulus*—about three cents.

210. A *pornikon telos* (brothel tax) was paid to the much dis-liked *pornotelonai* (brothel tax collectors).

211. The custom of the red lantern to identify a brothel was first established by law in Avignon, France, in 1234.

212. During the Tang dynasty (618–906 A.D.) Chinese houses of prostitution were recognized by the blue lanterns hung from the doorway, and were referred to as "blue houses."

213. The term "bordello" comes from the medieval French *bordel*, meaning "small house of boards."

214. Streets which contained brothels in fourteenth-century Southware, England, near London, bore such names as "Whore's Nest," "Slut's Hole," and "Gropecunt Lane." In fifteenth-century Paris, one could find similar streets named *Rue Puits d'Amour* (Whore's Hole Lane) and *Rue Poilecon* (Hairy-cunt Lane).

215. Sexual bathroom graffiti is not a modern custom. Excava-tion of the ruins of Pompeii, buried by the volcanic eruption of Mt. Vesuvius in 79 A.D., discovered walls barring two-thousand year-old obscene comments such as *"Hic ego puellas multas futui"* ("Here I fucked many girls") and *"Si qui futuere volet Atticen quaerat a XVI"* ("If you want to fuck, see Attica at No. 16").

216. The first female settlers of New Orleans were prostitutes and criminals. At the request of New Orleans founder Jean Baptiste le Moyne, Sieur de Bienville, who asked for women companions for his men, King Louis XV sent the entire inmate population of La Salpetriere Women's Prison to the new city. Not to be outdone, England sent twelve thousand female outcasts and

undesirables to the American colonies during the first half of the seventeenth century.

217. During the eighteenth and nineteenth centuries, and in Naples during World War II, it was not uncommon for impoverished families to sell their children into prostitution.

218. In mid-seventeenth-century London there were brothels that catered solely to pedophiles.

219. Seventeenth-century prostitutes were once called "nannies."

220. In the Japanese brothel district of Yoshiwara, young girls practiced "fluting" (fellatio), for it was considered demeaning for the cultured Geisha to do so.

221. Statistical estimates of the mid-1800s indicate there were approximately 6,000 brothels and 80,000 to 100,000 prostitutes working in metropolitan London.

222. High-class London prostitutes of the late 1800s were often referred to as "horse-breakers" because of their penchant for riding in the fashionable areas of the city.

223. Prostitution flourished in early nineteenth-century Vienna, and it was claimed that 20,000 out of a population of 400,000 were engaged in prostitution—one female for every seven or eight adult males. Between 6,000 and 7,000 women were hospitalized annually with venereal disease.

224. During the eighteenth and nineteenth centuries, guide books and directories to call houses, brothels, and prostitutes were available in many European and North American cities. *Les Bordels de Paris* (1790), London's "Hints to the Man About Town," and the notorious "New Orleans Blue Book" are a few of the more well-known publications.

225. During the Civil War, homosexuality was not uncommon

among the troops of both the North and the South, and male prostitutes were known to follow the armies.

226. Military outposts along the expanse of the Great Wall of China included a "barracks brothel." In addition to their regular duty of entertaining lonely men, government prostitutes were trained as reserve soldiers in the event of an attack by Mongolian hordes.

227. The notorious "Cowyards" of Reno and San Francisco in the 1800s were large buildings that contained over one hundred cribs used by prostitutes to service their customers. Each floor of the building contained different classes of prostitutes with the least expensive at the bottom and increasing in price with each successive floor. The four-hundred-bed Hotel Nymphia in San Francisco, which opened in 1899, had the added attraction of a small strategically placed window at each door, where, for a dime, potential patrons could view an unclad girl or watch the action going on inside.

228. Denver prostitutes of the late 1800s were referred to as "soiled doves," and were required to wear yellow ribbons.

229. Frontierswoman Martha Jane Canary Burke, better known as "Calamity Jane," was both patron and employee of western brothels. The daughter of a prostitute, she sought the company of whores while dressed as a man, and also worked as prostitute and madam throughout her life. The nickname "Calamity" was said to have come from the inevitable social disease she inflicted upon persons who had sex with her.

230. The term "Tenderloin District" came from the practice of corrupt vice police who accepted graft payment from prostitutes, pimps, and madams, enabling them to upgrade their regular diet of hamburger and cheap cuts of meat to expensive steaks.

231. It was alleged that President Warren G. Harding engaged in sexual trysts with his mistress, Nan Britton, in a five-foot by five-foot closet in an antechamber of the cabinet room.

232. Esther Cleveland, born September 9, 1893, was the first baby delivered at the White House. Her father, Grover Cleveland, was the first president to marry in the White House, taking a bride, Frances Folsom, on June 2, 1886.

233. On May 11, 1872, the colorful and outspoken Victoria C. Woodhull, suffragette, advocate of "free love," former spiritualist, and prostitute, announced her candidacy for president of the United States, representing the newly formed Equal Rights Party.

234. While interracial marriage was taboo, it was socially acceptable during the early seventeenth century for affluent Southern gentlemen of New Orleans to keep a light-skinned "colored" mistress. Important liaisons were often formed at the masked Quadroon Balls where attractive well-born mulatto, quadroon, or octoroon women could be introduced to wealthy white men.

235. An accepted marital custom of seventeenth-century Italian society was for a husband to provide his wife with a *cicisbeo*, a male escort, confidant, and lover.

236. To obtain a divorce in the 1920s, Russian citizens didn't need their spouse's consent. The party desiring the divorce merely notified the registrar's office, which in turn mailed a certificate of divorce to the other spouse. The period of the famous "divorce postcards" lasted until 1936, when new divorce laws were enacted.

237. Nighttime "panty raids" on sororities and women's dormitories became a popular fad among American male college students in the 1930s and 40s. Hordes of high-spirited young men would storm the buildings, ransacking drawers and seizing coeds' underwear.

238. A favored expression during World War II servicemen boasting of sexual conquest originated from the real-life sexual exploits of actor Errol Flynn. After a successful sexual encounter a G.I. would invariably remark, "In like Flynn."

SEX ... THEIR WAY!

Surprising Cultural Facts

Nowhere are the extremes and variety of human sexual expression more evident than when exploring the sexual practices that exist among global cultures. Sexual mores shaped by cultural attitudes can run the gamut from the sexually free and open Oceanic societies such as the Trobiands, to highly restrictive cultures like the isolated Irish community of Inis Beag, where the sexes are segregated for most of their lives. The concept of sex as an expression of love is certainly not universal; it may be a notion that is foreign or even absent in some societies. Reproduction can often be a violent, brutal affair for the sole purpose of producing offspring. While the rituals of some cultures may seem peculiar, barbaric, or even repulsive, it is likely that those same cultures view our "civilized" Western sexual practices with similar attitudes.

Due to the rapidly changing global cultural environment, the sexual customs found throughout the following chapter, while authenticated by numerous ethnographic studies, may or may not be currently practiced. The sexual practices of some preliterate societies have remained unchanged for hundreds of years, while others have been greatly influenced by the introduction of Western mores and sexual customs.

1. As part of their puberty rights, Ponapean males are required to undergo hemicastration (removal of one testis).

2. Among some African cultures such as the Masai, puberty

48

rituals include "female circumcision," or clitoridectomy (surgical removal of the clitoris).

3. Young Kenuzi Nubian girls are said to undergo removal of the clitoris at age four, and infibulation (suturing) of the vaginal opening.

4. It is claimed the Poro people of Liberia practice puberty rights in which the circumcised foreskin of the boy is exchanged for the excised clitoris and labia minora of the girl. As part of the ceremony of initiation the exchanged parts are cooked and eaten.

5. Former circumcision rites of the Bala tribe of Zaire once required the excised foreskin of a young boy to be wrapped in a banana leaf and placed on a termite hill to be eaten. The boy's father kept vigil at the spot until all remains were eaten; failure to do otherwise was thought to cause the boy to later become impotent.

6. During ceremonial rights of puberty in which circumcision of males is performed, the Australian Aborigines exchange wives as a gesture of friendship and goodwill.

7. Sodomy has been regularly practiced among the Keraki males of New Guinea, and at puberty all young boys were required to submit to anal and oral sex for a period of one year. After this rite of passage, they were then permitted to participate in the initiation of new pubescent males. The Keraki believe it is necessary for young boys to receive the semen of mature experienced warriors in order to properly develop into men, and failure to do so will leave them small, weak, and inferior.

8. Homosexual relationships are an accepted practice among all men and boys of the Siwans of Africa, and most engage in anal intercourse. The few who do not participate in homosexual liaisons are considered peculiar.

9. Believing that young boys could become pregnant as a

result of anal intercourse, the Keraki regularly performed a ceremony in which lime was eaten as a means of contraception.

10. Young Lenge girls of East Africa were required to be deflowered by a phallus made of horn as part of their ceremonial puberty rights.

11. The ceremony celebrating the first menstruation of a Bimin-Kuskuman girl includes a purification ritual that requires piercing of her nose, left earlobe, and extensive scarification by administration of over one hundred inch-long incisions on her abdomen.

12. Pendulous breasts are considered desirable among the Baganda, and young women of this culture are said to tie down, or apply weights to their breasts to obtain the desired effect.

13. The South American Siriono consider obese females attractive, especially if they possess fat on the mons and vulva.

14. The African Hottentots prize the female who has large fatty buttocks. Two medical conditions are named for this phenomenon—the "Hottentot bustle" (excessively fat buttocks) and "Hottentot apron" (elongated labia minora).

15. Young girls of Venda, in Northern Africa, and females of Benin, in Western Africa, are expected to rub and manipulate their labia to lengthen and enlarge them—a physical trait which the Venda male considers attractive.

16. The Ponapeans of the Eastern Caroline Islands also find the woman with an enlarged labia and clitoris attractive. It's claimed they employ old impotent men to beat, suck, and pull on the genitals to produce the desired results, and may also apply black ants, whose stinging will produce swelling of the genitals.

17. Nursing mothers of the Alorese Islands in Indonesia sometimes fondle or stroke an infant's genitals when it is suckling, and adults of the Kazak society in Central Asia have been known to

engage in genital play with children by manually stimulating them.

18. To quiet a fussy child, it is acceptable in some regions of the Philippines for mothers to caress their children's genitals.

19. Lesu children are permitted to watch adults, other than their parents, copulate.

20. An acceptable sexual practice among prepubescent members of the South African Bantu tribe is "metsha," a form of intercrural (between the thighs) intercourse.

21. The Ila people of Africa encourage their children to fully develop their sexual capabilities, permitting them any form sexual expression they wish to partake in. It is claimed that there are no virgins older than age ten in this society.

22. The inhabitants of the Trobriand Islands are reported to be the most sexually uninhibited and free among all known societies. Children are allowed to indulge in any type of sexual play, with intercourse occurring at an early age. All aspects of sex are considered natural, and adults and children alike are given free reign of their sexual desires.

23. In Polynesia, adolescents of both sexes are instructed in sexual techniques by an older experienced person, and during this period it is permissible to have numerous sexual liaisons before settling down to married life. Special "pleasure houses" are built to provide young people with their own place to socialize and have intercourse.

24. Upon reaching puberty, boys of Mangaia (one of the Cook Islands) are given sexual instruction and taught the technique of various coital positions, breast stimulation, cunnilingus, and the method for delaying ejaculation (*coitus reservatus*), so that their partners may experience multiple orgasms.

25. Although the Trobriand society is sexually permissive and tolerant of most forms of sexual expression and premarital inter-

course, its inhabitants, at one time, shared a universal ignorance and disbelief in the generative function of semen. It was believed that only the female was responsible for procreation.

26. Among some Oceanic societies, a young unwed girl who became pregnant was often considered a more desirable potential mate, having proven her fertility.

27. The Tahitian Ariori Society, said to have been founded by the fertility god Oro, has a membership of young single adults who travel among the neighboring tribes to perform at ceremonies and celebrations, providing entertainment in the form of singing, dancing, and sexual exhibitions.

28. Anthropologist George Murdock's 1949 survey of 158 societies revealed that 70 percent permitted premarital intercourse.

29. Of the ten insular Pacific societies, 90 percent condone premarital sex.

30. The National Center for Health statistics for 1988, reports that approximately 70 percent of married American women have had premarital intercourse, and that by age 25, 95 percent of American females have had sex.

31. The inhabitants of Tonga allow premarital intercourse with permission of the girl's parents and the provision that conception won't occur. Should pregnancy result, the offending couple must walk around the village naked for several days and apply a magic potion to the fence surrounding the community to prevent disease from infecting the population.

32. In some regions of the Philippines, engaged couples exchange soiled clothing which can be sniffed and fondled when the wearer is absent.

33. Among the tribes of the Otomacus of Venezuela, marriage between young people is prohibited. Older women marry young males and young girls are married to older men.

34. Samoan marriage rites include the use of a "marriage spoon," which is actually two half spoons whose handles are carved in the likeness of a naked female and naked male with an erection. The two halves of the spoon fit together in a manner that simulates copulation, forming one large spoon.

35. It is the custom of the Araucanos of Chile that the bridegroom must forcibly abduct the bride from her family, carrying her off by horseback to a hut in the woods.

36. The custom of carrying the bride over the threshold originated from societies which practiced "marriage by capture." Another popular theory proposed that it was an ancient practice which prevented evil spirits from entering the newlyweds' house.

37. In some regions of Italy it was the custom of a suitor to abduct and deflower a female, then offer to marry her.

38. Some Hindu sects require a priest to deflower a virgin before she consummates the marriage with her husband.

39. The most common universal form of marriage is polygyny, (one husband with two or more wives). Anthropologist George Murdock's Ethnographic Atlas claims that of 849 societies, 70 percent are polygynous. Polygyny may not be as widely practiced today as it once was because of the prohibitive cost of keeping more than one wife.

40. The least prevalent form of marriage is polyandry, (one wife with two or more husbands). Only 4 of 849 societies are polyandrous.

41. There are many variations of sexual expression, though heterosexual intercourse remains the most prevalent form among all human societies.

42. The West African Fon, of Benin, have thirteen different forms of marriage including one in which a female adopts the male role, taking a wife, or in some cases, wives. By agreement a male may be contracted to impregnate his wife, promising to

deny any paternal or economic rights to the offspring. A similar form of same-sex female marriage is practiced among tribes of southern Bantu, although these unions are mostly ceremonial in nature and not sexually consummated.

43. Polyandry is practiced by the Toda of India. When a female marries she also becomes wife to her husband's brothers, establishing a sexual relationship with all of them.

44. While incestuous relationships are prohibited among the general population of most societies, some specific cultures, such as the Azande of Africa, require the high chiefs to marry their own daughters, ensuring the continuation of a royal lineage.

45. The Toda of India have no word for adultery in their language, moreover, it is acceptable for both men and women to have lovers or extramarital relationships.

46. The vocabulary of Polynesian societies have no words for "obscene," "indecent," or "impure." Sex is never considered a source of shame or embarrassment.

47. The highly moralistic society of Inis Beag, off the coast of Ireland, is so sexually repressive that the sexes are segregated both before and after marriage. Premarital sex and discussion of sexual topics is taboo. Basic sexual physiology and female orgasm are virtually unknown, and sex is furtively performed for the sole purpose of procreation. It is thought that the male sex drive is a result of eating too many potatoes, a dietary staple of the island.

48. The Bimin-Kuskusmin, an agricultural society, maintain separate "male" and "female" crops which are ritually fertilized with semen and menstrual blood respectively.

49. The North African Siwa man believes a woman will find him irresistible if he surreptitiously laces her food with his semen.

50. Because eating and intercourse each involve entering bodi-

ly orifices, the Aweikoma of southeastern Brazil use the same term for both activities.

51. The Mundurucu', an Amazoanian tribe, refer to sexual intercourse as "eating penises."

52. The term "missionary position" originated among Oceanic people such as the Trobriand Islanders, who were urged by missionaries to adopt the "man on top" position as the only morally acceptable way to have intercourse. This position, uncommon to their society, was a source of amusement, as well as the belief that their more preferred positions and sexual variations were sinful and heathenlike.

53. It's claimed that the women of the island of Lesu invite sexual advances by displaying their genitals to their intended lover.

54. Should a Kurtatchi woman of the Solomon Islands unintentionally reveal her genitals, she may be subject to sexual assault by any nearby male.

55. If a woman of the Mehinaku indian tribe of central Brazil dares enter the sacred men's house, she will be taken to the woods and gang-raped.

56. The inhabitants of Bali, and the Lepcha of Sikkim, have no elaborate practices of seduction. If sex is desired, one need only ask for it. This may be true equally of both men or women, although it is less acceptable for Lepcha women to solicit intercourse.

57. Jaluit men in the Marshall Islands invite sex by rolling their eyes and uttering the name of the genitals.

58. Western Australian Yungar men solicit intercourse by sending the object of their desire a carved stick smeared with yellow clay at one end.

59. It's been the tribal custom of New Guinea females to wear

the severed finger of their lover's war conquest as a necklace ornament.

60. Among the Kwoma of New Guinea it's considered proper for the girl to make sexual advances rather than the boy, who feels he might unintentionally anger the girl's parents.

61. If a Goajiro woman of Colombia is successful in tripping a man during a ceremonial dance, he is required to have intercourse with her.

62. Prior to intercourse, men and women of the Siriono tribe of eastern Bolivia engage in reciprocal delousing and grooming of their bodies. They indulge in a precopulatory snack of lice and wood ticks which are picked off the body and eaten.

63. While grooming is considered a type of foreplay resulting in intercourse, kissing, breast stimulation, or caressing prior to copulation is not practiced among the Siriono.

64. The Tinquian people of the Pacific islands do not kiss, but place their lips closely to their partner's and rapidly inhale.

65. The Balinese also do not kiss, but gently rub their faces together with slight movements of the head, enjoying the tactile sensation, and inhaling each other's scent.

66. It's claimed that as a type of foreplay, the Ponapean man may sometimes place a fish in the woman's vulva, gently licking it out prior to coitus.

67. While rear-entry intercourse is the predominate form of copulation for most mammals, there is no known human society where this is the preferred or most prevalent sexual position.

68. Males of the island of Tikopia, near the Solomons, are prohibited from touching their own or their partner's genitals. Insertion of the penis is usually assisted by the female.

69. Trobriand Islanders of the South Pacific engage in *mit-*

akuku, a practice in which a sexual partner's eyelashes and eyebrows are bitten off during lovemaking.

70. Sexual encounters among the South American Siriono, and also the Pacific Trobrianders, are often extremely physical and violent. Considerable biting, scratching, and hair-pulling may occur, escalating as climax approaches. "Battle scars" are proudly displayed as evidence of a successful sexual liaison.

71. Pacific-dwelling Marquesan men have acquired the ability to prolong their erections indefinitely until their partner is fully satisfied. It is considered desirable for women to experience two or three orgasms during prolonged intercourse.

72. Men of the Western Caroline Islands are said to sing to their partners before and after intercourse.

73. Men in regions of the Philippines and Borneo may use an *ampalling* to increase the sexual pleasure of their partner. A hole is incised into the penis and kept patent by insertion of a dove feather covered with oil. After healing has occurred a small rod approximately two inches in length made of ivory or gold may be inserted into the perforation just prior to intercourse. The top of the rod has a knob which is left exposed and used for sexual stimulation of the female.

74. Patagonian Indians employ a ringlike device called a *guesquel*, fashioned from the course stiff hair of the mule. It fits around the circumference of the penis, and its use during coitus is said to produce intense orgasms in women.

75. To increase a female's sexual pleasure some Southeast Asian males insert small gold or silver nuggets under the epidermis of the penis via an incision. These "tickling stones" are thought to provide added stimulation during intercourse. Burmese men are said to sometimes insert tiny bells instead of stones, which make a tinkling sound when they walk.

76. Among the Zapotec Indians of the Oaxaca Sierras, it is

considered a gesture of hospitality to offer an overnight guest one's wife or unmarried daughter.

77. When traveling to another tribe, the Chukchee man of Siberia is permitted to have intercourse with the host's wife. By mutual agreement, this form of hospitality will be reciprocated by the guest, should his host pay him a visit at a later time.

78. Many societies such as the Venezuelan Llan Indians, Brazilian Caingang, and Bolivian Siriono, permit sexual relations between one's siblings and spouse. A husband is allowed intercourse with his wife's sisters, and a wife may have similar sexual access to her husband's brothers.

79. During the latter stages of a Hidatsa woman's pregnancy, her husband is allowed intercourse with her sister.

80. The Abipon people practice three years of sexual abstinence between married couples following the birth of a child. Trobriand Islanders adhere to similar sexual restrictions for more than two years.

81. Giving birth on the New Guinea coastal island of Normbanby is a community affair, taking place in the center of the village and witnessed by all of the inhabitants.

82. The French term *couvade*, meaning "to hatch," or "to lie down," is a phenomenon documented in many South American, African, and Oceanic societies, and characterized by symptoms of pregnancy experienced by expectant fathers. Many primitive cultures require a husband to observe a period of confinement during the birth and postpartum phase.

83. "Doing the month" is a postpartum Chinese ritual that new mothers observe by convalescing in bed for thirty days. During this period they must eat chicken daily and are prohibited from bathing or washing their hair, fearing that any contact with water will later cause chronic ailments such as asthma and arthritis.

84. To reestablish good health following the delivery of a

baby, rural Malaysian females are subjected to a ceremonial "mother roasting," a ritual that requires the new mother to lie upon a *salaian*, a simple wood framed "roasting bed" placed over a small wood fire.

85. It's not uncommon for the Aranda of Australia to copulate three to five times nightly, sleeping for short intervals between periods of sexual activity.

86. The Siriono have intercourse outdoors every afternoon.

87. The Gond Tribe, of the Central Provinces in India, copulate in the bush, fearing that it will offend the "goddess of wealth" to have sex in one's dwelling where valuables are kept. Sexual transgression may result in economic misfortune and poverty.

88. The Masai of Africa have sex only at night, believing that intercourse during daylight hours will cause the male's blood to flow into the womb of the woman, leaving only water in his veins.

89. The nomadic Chenchu Tribe of Hyderabad, India, routinely copulate during the day, fearing that a child conceived in darkness will be born blind.

90. Upon the death of a family member, the Jivaro people of South America prohibit intercourse for all close relatives of the deceased for several days.

91. Men of the Western Caroline Islands who serve as pallbearers must abstain from sex for four days.

92. The Chewa of Central Africa require entire families to refrain from intercourse if one of their members is ill.

93. Inhabitants of the island of Kiwai, off the southeastern coast of New Guinea, believe it is bad luck to have sex the night before a hunting expedition or journey.

94. Males in Thailand are offered free vasectomies on the

king's birthday—over one thousand are performed annually in his honor.

95. In some Arab and Islamic countries it is the custom of men who engage in migratory labor to require their wives to infibulate (suture shut) their genitals to ensure fidelity. This procedure is performed in such a way as to allow the passage of urine and menstrual flow, but prevent sexual intromission.

96. In Kafa in southwestern Ethiopia, a man found guilty of violating a virgin may be punished by having his head or hands cut off.

97. In some Islamic countries women may be executed for committing adultery, though traditionally, men receive only a light punishment. In Saudi Arabia, adultery is a capital offense punishable by death from stoning.

98. The Serni of Brazil punish the adulterous wife by whipping her, then exposing the wounds to stinging fire ants.

99. It's claimed that within the last decade 25 percent (over eighty thousand females) of the female population of Addis Ababa, Ethiopia, have engaged in prostitution.

100. Generational prostitution was practiced by the inhabitants of the Santa Cruz Islands. Infanticide was commonly performed on male infants born to prostitutes, while female infants were raised to assume the occupation of their mothers.

101. In the wake of the AIDS epidemic, child prostitution has increased dramatically in Asian countries such as Thailand, Taiwan, and the Philippines, driven by client demand for disease-free virgins.

102. Some societies, such as the Chukchee of Siberia, permit homosexuality and transvestism. The male who dresses like a woman and assumes the female role is referred to as a *berdache*, and is allowed to have a male spouse.

103. The Tanala of Madagascar refer to effeminate or homosexual men as *sarombavy*.

104. At one time, specially selected male children among the Alaskan Koniag were raised as females from infancy, eventually becoming the wife of a chief or tribal leader. A similar custom of aboriginal tribes in Greenland designate this person an *Achnutshik*.

105. Homosexuality is an accepted practice among the South American Lache and Caquiteros. Homosexual marriages are not uncommon; moreover, women who have borne five sons are permitted to raise one of them as a female.

106. Among the African Benin and Nama tribes, the only acceptable form of homosexuality is mutual masturbation.

107. Homosexual relations among Chukchee women of Siberia may include the use of an artificial penis fashioned from the large dried calf muscle of the reindeer.

108. The Azande of eastern Sudan permit female homosexual relations, and they are reported to use such items as carved wooden phalli, bananas, manioc, or sweet potatoes as penis substitutes.

109. Lesu women do not use their hands for masturbation. In the absence of a partner, it is an accepted practice to sit in a position with the right leg bent, enabling the heel of the foot to press against the genitals.

110. In an effort to save its rapidly declining herds of rhinoceros the government of Zimbabwe has started a program to surgically remove their horns, which fetch up to $12,000 on the black market. Poachers have long catered to the Oriental demand for powdered Rhinoceros horn, used by Asians as an aphrodisiac.

111. North American poachers are paid $400 to $600 for the gallbladder of the black bear, another sought-after aphrodisiac in the Far East.

112. *Koro*, meaning "shrinking tortoise," a psychological phenomenon seen almost exclusively in Asian and Oceanic cultures, is characterized by a sudden irrational fear that the victim's penis is shrinking and disappearing into his abdomen, and is accompanied by a feeling of impending death.

113. The ancient Japanese Kanayama Shrine, erected to offer charms and prayers to the gods for protection from venereal disease, has spawned a brisk trade in a new talisman which features three monkeys displaying the familiar "hear no evil, see no evil" sign, with the addition of two monkeys with strategically placed hands over their genitals. This new token is said to provide protection from AIDS to those who attach it to the altar.

114. Practitioners of the Tantric sect of Hinduism strive to achieve a transcendental state by using specific Tantric yoga positions for intercourse, prolonging the act to the threshold of orgasm without climax or ejaculation in the belief that higher consciousness can be attained by redirecting the sexual energy of the genitals throughout the body to the brain.

115. If a Chinese bride follows the traditional marriage customs, she will wear a red wedding costume.

116. The Chinese feudal ceremony *yin pei* (wedding after death) is still practiced sporadically in some provinces. It is a custom that allows a young deceased person to be married to another deceased person, providing them a mate in the afterlife. Sometimes an embalmed body may be kept for years until an eligible spouse-corpse is available for marriage.

SEX . . . OUR WAY!

The Incredible Spectrum

Sexually speaking—where is our society at these days? This final chapter is devoted to exploring American sexual trends, ranging from teen sex, AIDS, sex crime, and abortion to marriage, reproduction, and current sexual habits. Some of the facts are surprising, some even alarming.

The "baby boom" generation began setting the trend when their parents gave birth to the largest number of babies ever recorded in one year (1960). Thirty years later, while in their peak childbearing years, the "boomers" were nearly able to match that record with the second largest number of recorded births in 1990.

Today, every minute in the United States three teenagers become pregnant and one gives birth, three abortions are performed, twenty-three people contact a sexually transmitted disease, five people become infected with the AIDS virus, and there are two AIDS-related deaths. There are also four marriages, seven births, and two divorces. Every five minutes a U.S. female is raped. Among industrialized nations, the United States continues to lead the world—with the highest annual rate of teenage births, number of teen abortions, and infant mortality.

Except for the invention of the birth control pill in the 1950s, the discovery of the AIDS virus in 1980 has had the greatest impact on sexuality of any event in our era, affecting the sexual habits of millions of people worldwide.

1. In April 1970, Gloria Sykes of Dearborn Heights, Michi-

gan, was awarded a $50,000 judgment against the San Francisco Railway for injuries she sustained in a cable car accident. In addition to two black eyes and several bruises, she claimed that trauma from the accident had caused her to become a nymphomaniac, and that she once had sex fifty times within a period of 5 days.

2. The origin of the word "nymphomania" is from the Greek *nymphe* (bride) and *mania* (madness or frenzy).

3. S.L.A.A. (Sex and Love Addicts Anonymous), a support group for individuals who suffer from compulsive or pathological sexual behavior, was founded in 1976 in Cambridge, Massachusetts, and is based on the A.A. twelve-step recovery plan.

4. There has been a dramatic increase of infidelity among married women since the 1940s Kinsey Report which revealed that 26 percent of married women were unfaithful. Forty percent of wives over age forty who were polled by the 1977 Redbook Report on Female Sexuality admitted a sexual infidelity, while a 1986 national survey of 2,000 women age twenty-five to fifty, by Thor Data of New York City, found that of the 36 percent of respondents who were married, 41 percent had admitted cheating on their husbands. The Morton Hunt survey for *Playboy* magazine, which polled 100,000 adults, reported that among its married female respondents who were employed full time, 40 percent had engaged in sex outside their marriage, compared to an incidence of 20 percent among nonworking wives.

5. It was reported in *Almanac of the American People* that among couples who had been married ten or more years, 30 percent of husbands and 22 percent of wives had been unfaithful to their spouse.

6. The Hunt survey also showed a surprising relationship between income and the incidence of infidelity. Only 16 percent of husbands who earned less than $5,000 a year had engaged in

extramarital sex, while 70 percent of husbands earning over $60,000 a year had done so.

7. When a single woman has an affair with a married man, there is a 70 percent likelihood that the man will be the one to end it.

8. While rarely enforced, adultery laws currently exist in thirty-seven states. Twelve states have never passed adultery or fornication laws.

9. In June 1990, three Connecticut people were arrested in two separate incidents and charged with adultery, a misdemeanor crime punishable by a maximum sentence of one year in prison and a $1,000 fine.

10. The United States has more laws governing sexual behavior than all of the European nations combined. The only legally sanctioned sexual act in the United States is private heterosexual intercourse between married adults.

11. Many states have statutes which prohibit the mating or copulation of domestic animals such as horses, sheep, or pigs, within a specific distance of a school, church, or residential area.

12. A twenty-five-year study by A. W. Richards, a Maryland psychotherapist and former priest, found that nearly 50 percent of Catholic priests break their vows of celibacy.

13. There are currently over fifty married Catholic priests practicing in the United States. Since 1981, the Roman Catholic Church has allowed married Episcopal ministers who choose to convert to Catholicism to be reordained.

14. A survey by Masters and Johnson revealed that "heterosexual" encounters were the third most frequent fantasy theme of both male and female homosexuals.

15. The 1974 (pre-AIDS) Bell Survey of male homosexual

promiscuity claimed that the average number of sexual partners in the lifetime of a gay man was one thousand.

16. More than 25 percent of American males have had intimate sexual contact with another male during their lifetime. Kinsey's research estimates that 30 percent of all U.S. males have experienced a homosexual encounter.

17. The most common sexual activity among homosexuals is fellatio.

18. Masters and Johnson report that three males per one thousand perform self-fellatio.

19. As many as one in four women and one in six men may have been victims of familial sexual abuse.

20. Annually, over sixty thousand American children are sexually abused by a family member.

21. During their lifetimes, fifty percent of U.S. women and 15 percent of U.S. men will be victims of sexual assault.

22. Less than 10 percent of violent sexual crime is actually reported to police, and fewer than one in sixty sexual crimes result in an arrest.

23. In 1990, 290 women were arrested and charged with rape; 76 of those females were under the age of eighteen.

24. The U.S. Department of Justice reports that in 1990, 435 children between the ages of ten and twelve were arrested for forcible rape, and another 2,562 for sex offenses (other than prostitution).

25. More than 289 rapes occur every day in the United States— about one rape every five minutes.

26. The largest number of forcible rapes usually occur in the month of July and are typically committed in the victim's home

(25 percent), at night (58 percent), and involve a weapon (26 percent).

27. The U.S. Department of Justice 1990 crime index revealed that among American universities and colleges, Indiana's Ball State University had the highest number of reported forcible rapes.

28. A 1987 study of 561 sex offenders participating in a treatment program found that the typical rapist had previously committed over seven rapes, and the average child molester, 282 sexual assaults involving 150 juvenile victims.

29. Sexual offenders are often found to have below-average knowledge of basic sexual anatomy and sexual functioning.

30. Data from the U.S. Bureau of Justice Statistics revealed that the average length of incarceration of rapists is three years.

31. As an alternative to a lengthy sentence, the Canadian government, in 1976, offered convicted rapists the option of voluntary castration.

32. There were more forcible rapes (162 per 100,000 population) committed in Atlanta in 1989 than in any other large U.S. metropolitan city. Second place went to Cleveland with 160. The safest streets for women were found in Washington, D.C. (31), followed by San Diego (37).

33. When surveyed about activities which are deemed "sinful" or "immoral," respondents of the 1986 "Religion in America" Gallup Poll said that on a scale of one to ten, they rated "sexual abuse of children" (9.92) the second most sinful activity. Number one was murder—9.94, third was "rape" (9.70), and fourth, "lying about a sexual disease" (9.68). Of the sixty-one activities, they rated "masturbation" the least sinful (2.22).

34. It's estimated that more than 85 percent of U.S. females have engaged in masturbation at some time in their life.

35. A survey in 1980 indicated there were approximately thirty-five legal brothels in Nevada. Prostitution is permitted only in Nevada towns which have a population of less than 200,000.

36. Legalized prostitution is strictly regulated by the Nevada counties and municipalities that allow it, and ordinances include such restrictions as prohibiting women from leaving their house of employment on Sunday, or daily between the hours of 6 p.m. and 10 a.m., entering a bar, casino, or residential area, or no more than three prostitutes visiting town at the same time.

37. Prostitution in Nevada was not legalized until 1974. Missouri had the distinction, in 1872, of being the first state to have legalized prostitution by requiring St. Louis brothelkeepers and workers to register with the city, and adhere to specific laws regulating their trade. In 1897 Louisiana followed suit, when, at the suggestion of Alderman Sidney Story, the city of New Orleans created the district of "Storyville" where prostitution trade was lawfully permitted.

38. While there is little disagreement over the origins of jazz, there has been considerable speculation about the etymology of the word itself. One popular theory is that the improvisational music born in the nightclubs and brothels of the red light district of New Orleans during the late nineteenth century was named for the favored slang for sex—"jazz."

39. The early clinical research of sexual response by Masters and Johnson was conducted with the cooperation of 118 prostitutes.

40. In Fairbanks, during the mid-1970s construction of the Alaskan Pipeline, arrests for prostitution increased 4,000 percent.

41. A twenty-year study of over one thousand female prostitutes by the El Paso County Health Department found that the average working girl will remain in her profession about five years.

42. There are currently over 1 million full-time female prostitutes working in the United States.

43. A recent survey of prostitutes revealed that the most frequent sex act performed is fellatio.

44. There are over twenty known sexually transmitted diseases (STDs).

45. There are seven different malignancies of the reproductive organs that are associated with STDs.

46. The Centers for Disease Control (CDC) estimate that over 12 million cases of STD occur annually—that's nearly 23 per minute.

47. According to the National Center for Health Statistics, 50 percent of single men age twenty-five who have been sexually active since their teens have contracted at least one STD.

48. Among sexually active adults, lesbians have the lowest incidence of STD.

49. The most prevalent and fastest-growing STD in the United States is chlamydia, with nearly 5 million cases reported annually.

50. Current statistics from the Centers for Disease Control (CDC), indicate that among sexually transmitted diseases such as gonorrhea, syphilis, genital herpes, and genital warts, AIDS is the least prevalent.

51. Pubic crab lice *(Phthirus pubis)*, called *Papillon d'Amour* ("Butterfly of Love") by the French, can survive only twenty-four hours after leaving the body, although their eggs can survive for six days.

52. "Vanilla" derives its name from the Latin word for vagina, probably because of the vanilla bean's likeness to female genitalia.

53. Sexual "paraphilias" are classified as a deviation characterized by sexual arousal from specific objects or situations such as telephone scatologia (obscene language), necrophilia (corpses), partialism (obsession with a particular body part), zoophilia (animals), coprophilia (feces), klismaphilia (enemas), urophilia (urine), and frottage (rubbing genitals against a stranger in a crowed place). Some of the more unusual paraphilias might include gerontophilia (preferred sexual attraction to an elderly adult), infantilism (sexual pleasure derived from engaging in activities associated with infant care, such as diapering), symphorophilia (sexual arousal from experiencing an accident or catastrophe), and acrotomophilia, Greek for *acro* "extremity" and *tomo* "cut" (a sexual preference for amputees)

54. You are a "phylogynist" if you love or like women.

55. If you have a fear of men, you may suffer from "androphobia."

56. A "parthenologist" specializes in the study of virgins and virginity.

57. The origin of the word "hysteria" is from the Greek *hysterikos* or *hystero*, meaning "uterus." Classified as a strictly female disorder in the nineteenth century, it was thought to be a manifestation of repressed sexuality or inadequate sexual outlet.

58. The clinical term for masochistic and sadistic sexual behavior is "algolagnia" (sexual pleasure derived from receiving or inflicting pain).

59. Sexual variation or deviant behavior such as fetishism, exhibitionism, voyeurism, or zoophilia is primarily and almost exclusively a male proclivity. True female deviates are rare.

60. Sex offenders who are exhibitionists are most likely to be married men.

61. In Britain, the act of stealing a woman's underpants by a fetishist is called "knicker picking."

62. Statistical data gathered by the American Psychiatric Association for the DSM-III-R (Diagnostic and Statistical Manual of Mental Disorders, 1987), revealed that approximately 8 percent of young adult males have Male Erectile Disorder, 30 percent suffer from Premature Ejaculation, 30 percent of the female population have Inhibited Female Orgasm, and 20 percent of the total population suffers from Hypoactive Sexual Desire Disorder.

63. A recent survey of mental health professionals reported that the most frequent complaints of clients were associated with marital dissatisfaction and lack of intimacy, whereas the eighth most common complaint was about sex.

64. It's estimated that between 5 percent and 13 percent of physicians and mental health professionals have had sexual contact with their patients, and that 5 percent have engaged in sexual intercourse with patients.

65. According to Daniel Evan Weiss, author of *100% American*, for variety, 19 percent of American wives choose the outdoors as an alternative location for sex.

66. Mr. Weiss also states that 4 percent of American women own no undergarments, and that 6 percent of them sleep in the nude.

67. Sixty-six percent of runners surveyed by Harper's Index claimed they thought about sex while running, while 8 percent of the respondents said they thought about running while engaged in sex.

68. *The Guinness Book of World Records* reports that the record for the most children born to a mother during her lifetime is sixty-nine. The wife of Feodor Vassilyev, a Russian peasant, gave birth to four sets of quadruplets, seven sets of triplets, and sixteen sets of twins; sixty-seven of those children survived infancy

69. Twins occur about 1 in 100 births, triplets 1 in 10,000, quadruplets 1 in 1,000,000, and quintuplets 1 in 90,000,000.

70. Twins are typically delivered about 10 minutes apart.

71. The term "Siamese twins" originated with the birth, in 1843, of Chang and Eng Bunker, who were joined at the chest. Though actually of Chinese descent, their congenital disorder was named for their birthplace, Siam (Thailand). As adults, they married the Yates sisters of Wilkes County, North Carolina, and between them fathered a total of twenty-two children. Incidentally, their names, Chang and Eng, literally mean "left" and "right."

72. The record for the oldest mother to give birth was authenticated October 18, 1956, when fifty-seven-year-old Mrs. Ruth Alice Kistler gave birth in Glendale, California, to a daughter, Suzan.

73. The U.S. Bureau of Census states that 44,001 babies were born to American mothers between the ages of forty and forty-four in 1989. Nearly 1,600 babies were born to women age forty-five or older.

74. Women thirty-five years and older have the greatest number of cesarean deliveries.

75. The largest number of live births in the United States occurred in 1960 (during the "baby boom"), with over 4,257,850 recorded that year. Interestingly, as the "boomers" reached peak childbearing age, they contributed to the second largest number of recorded births (4,146,000) in 1990.

76. The number of U.S. babies born in 1988 who *were not* delivered in a hospital is 37,000.

77. Prior to World War I only poor, indigent, or unwed mothers gave birth in hospitals; upper- and middle-class women preferred the comforts of their home, attended by their physician or midwife. At the turn of the century fewer than 10 percent of

females delivered in hospitals, though by 1955 more than 90 percent did so.

78. Jimmy Carter was the first U.S. president to be born in a hospital. He was born October 1, 1924 at Wise Sanitarium in Plains, Georgia.

79. October 28, 1929, Mrs. T. W. Evans, a passenger on a transport plane, gave birth to the first U.S. baby born in an airplane, while flying over Miami, Florida.

80. The Volkswagen company has awarded over five hundred savings bonds to babies born in its cars.

81. More babies will be born to parents between the ages of twenty-five and twenty-nine than any other age group.

82. Nearly 25 percent of all U.S. babies are delivered by cesarean section.

83. The largest documented live birth weight of a baby is 22 pounds, 8 ounces. Only two such births are recorded—to an Italian mother in 1955 and a South African mother in 1982.

84. The largest tumor ever recorded was a 325-pound ovarian cyst, removed from a Texas woman in 1905. Despite the tumor's size, she had a successful recovery. The removal of a similarly large ovarian tumor from a Chicago woman in 1951 resulted in the official world record for the longest surgery, which lasted four days and reduced the weight of the patient from 616 to 308 pounds.

85. The world record for the most bigamous marriages is held by Giovanni Vigliotto of Syracuse, Sicily, who was arrested on December 30, 1981 in Panama City, Florida. He was later convicted of 104 fraudulent marriages in more than twenty-seven states and fourteen countries, spanning over a period of forty-one years. Incredulously, he married four of his victims while aboard a cruise ship in 1968.

86. The largest mass wedding ever recorded was performed on October 30, 1988, by Reverend Sun Myung Moon, head of the Unification Church, who married 6,516 couples in Seoul, South Korea.

87. In 1984 there were 2,477,000 marriages—the largest number ever recorded. The most divorces occurred in 1981 with 1,213,000.

88. Alaska and Utah are the states with the highest birth rates.

89. Oral-genital sex (cunnilingus and fellatio), has long been a preferred form of sexual variation in Western society. Its wide acceptance is supported by numerous surveys; from the Kinsey reports of the 40s and 50s which found that 60 percent of college-educated couples engaged in oral sex, to the 1974 Hunt survey which revealed that 90 percent of married couples under twenty-five enjoyed oral-genital lovemaking, regardless of educational level. Of the ten thousand married female respondents of the 1976 *Redbook* survey, and the women aged eighteen to thirty-four who were polled by *Cosmopolitan* in 1981, 85 percent said they engaged often in both cunnilingus and fellatio.

90. The *Redbook* survey also revealed that 2 percent of women enjoy using feathers for sexual stimulation, and that 9 percent masturbate while their partner watches.

91. What were 371,000 people doing in 1989 when, according to the National Safety Council, they reported injuries related to a bed, mattress, pillow, or bed linen?

92. In 1990 more than six thousand people reported injuries related to feminine hygiene products.

93. Desmond Morris, author of *The Naked Ape*, suggests that the female custom of wearing red lipstick is an unconscious desire to attract the opposite sex by mimicking the redness of the genital labia.

94. 1979 data from the Population Council, which supplied a global comparison of abortion rates per 1,000 women aged fifteen to forty-four, found that the former Soviet Union had the highest number (180), and West Germany the lowest (6.2). Of the ten countries surveyed, the United States was fourth, with 30.2.

95. There were 1,590,800 abortions performed in the United States in 1988 (that's over 4,358 per day). Of the fifty states, California performed the most abortions (312,000), and Wyoming the least (600).

96. Approximately 82 percent of abortions are performed on unmarried women.

97. More than twenty-six percent of U.S. women wishing to terminate a pregnancy are seeking their second abortion.

98. Ten percent of abortions in 1987 were performed on women beyond thirteen weeks gestation.

99. The ratio of live births to abortions in the United States is 1000:400. The ratio in the state of New York is 1000:634.

100. Although unavailable in the United States, RU 486, the "abortion pill" invented by French physician Etienne-Emile Baulieu, has proved 95 percent effective among the 55,000 women (in 15 countries) who have used it.

101. In May 1991, the U.S. Supreme Court prohibited federally-funded family planning clinics from discussing abortion—even if a client specifically requests the information.

102. Research conducted by the National Institute of Child Health and Human Development found the average age at which boys first engage in intercourse is 15.7 years.

103. Before marrying for the first time, the average single man will have had ten sexual partners. Fifty percent of single women

will have had fewer than four sexual partners prior to their first marriage.

104. Twelve percent of U.S. teens had their first sexual intercourse in an automobile.

105. Fewer than 30 percent of parents in the U.S. discuss sex with their children.

106. Less than 30 percent of U.S. junior and senior high schools provide a sex education curriculum.

107. The CDC estimates that 3 million American teenagers annually will contract a sexually transmitted disease—that's over five cases per minute.

108. An American teen becomes pregnant every twenty seconds, and gives birth every 1.7 minutes.

109. Teenage mothers delivered over 30 percent of U.S. babies born to unmarried females in 1988.

110. More babies are born to American teens than to those in any other industrialized nation in the Western Hemisphere.

111. Nearly 50 percent of pregnant unwed teens age fifteen to nineteen will choose to have an abortion, and they will represent over 25 percent of all legal abortions performed annually.

112. Children of mothers who married young and/or were pregnant before marriage are more likely to do the same.

113. Over 25 percent of American babies were born to unmarried women in 1988.

114. Unmarried mothers delivered 61 percent of the babies born in Washington, D.C., in 1988. The infant mortality (23.2 deaths per 1000 live births) in D.C. is more than twice the national average.

115. Among industrialized nations, the U.S. has the highest infant mortality rate (10.4), a figure that is more than double that

of Japan (4.5). (Figures based on the number of infant deaths per 1,000 live births.)

116. The current median age for a first marriage is 25.9 for men, and 23.6 for women—little change in over a century, when the median age in 1890 was 26.1 for men, and 22.0 for women.

117. Newborn, white babies weigh more today than they did thirty years ago. The average birth weight has increased three ounces from seven pounds, six ounces in 1960 to seven pounds, nine ounces in 1990.

118. American senior citizens enjoy sex. According to the 1980 Starr and Weiner survey of eight hundred men and women over sixty, 89% continued to be sexually active, and 40 percent of those in their eighties reported that they still enjoyed sexual relations. A similar study in 1981, by Linda George, found that those who were most sexually active in their younger years were most likely to continue to enjoy sex as they grew older.

119. There are currently about 100,000 unmarried couples in the United States age sixty-five or older.

120. A recent poll of American women found that 37 percent who claimed they "always enjoy sex" were typically childless, college educated, and earned over $25,000 a year.

121. A 1988–89 survey of fifteen hundred households, conducted by Tom Smith of the University of Chicago, revealed that American adults have sex an average of fifty-seven times a year, or about once a week. Another current poll of three thousand U.S. adults claimed the average was two to three times per week.

122. According to the National Center for Health Statistics & Vital Statistics of the U.S., the average marriage lasts twenty-three years. If this information is correct, then the typical couple can expect to have sex between 1,311 and 3,588 times during their married life—an average of 2,450.

123. If each act of intercourse lasts fifteen minutes, the average

couple will enjoy approximately 610 hours of connubial bliss during their married lives.

124. If that same couple each burn one hundred calories during lovemaking, they may eat two thousand calories for 122 days to replace the amount of energy expended.

125. Minnesotan Alfred Wolfram holds the official world record for kissing, after bussing 8,001 women in eight hours at the 1990 Minnesota Renaissance Festival.

126. Mel Poretz and Barry Sinrod, authors of *Do You Do It With the Lights On?*, estimate that 65 percent of women and 55 percent of men have, at least once, used a rest room designated for the opposite sex.

127. Sixty-six percent of pet owners surveyed by Poretz and Sinrod claimed that they allowed their pets to remain in the bedroom during lovemaking.

128. If you flunked the Sexual Trivia Challenge, take comfort in knowing you're not alone. Of the 1,974 individuals who participated in the 1989 Kinsey Institute test of basic sexual knowledge, only 5 people were able to answer correctly 95 percent of the eighteen questions asked. Over half of the test-takers (55 percent) answered incorrectly 50 percent or more of the questions.

129. The question most frequently missed (80 percent) by the Kinsey test-takers asked for the correct estimate of the percent of U.S. females who have engaged in anal intercourse (30 to 40 percent).

130. The 1987 "Annual Study of Women's Attitudes" revealed that, of its female respondents who were of childbearing age, 5 percent abstain from sex.

131. The Equal Employment Opportunity Commission receives over 4,500 complaints of sexual harassment yearly.

132. On July 1, 1971, Washington became the first state to enact

a law banning sex discrimination, making it illegal to refuse employment of a person solely on the basis of gender.

133. The California "McMartin Pre-School" sexual molestation case resulted in the longest and costliest trial in U.S. history. Despite seven years of court time (1983–1990) and cost of $13.5 million, the juries of two separate trials reached deadlocked decisions. A defendant in that case, Raymond Buckey, spent more that five years in jail awaiting the conclusion of the trial and a verdict.

134. Lewis Caroll, author of the children's classic *Alice in Wonderland*, was reported to have female pedophilic tendencies and was fond of entertaining and photographing prepubescent girls, sometimes posing them nude.

135. It's claimed that before fame as an author, Horatio Alger was forced to resign as minister of a Unitarian Church in Brewster, Massachusetts, in 1864 after he acknowledged having homosexual relations with two parishioners' sons.

136. On January 16, 1987, KRON of San Francisco became the first television station to air condom commercials.

137. Sales of condoms to women have increased 150 percent in the last decade.

138. It is estimated that over 1,000,000 condoms are sold in the United States daily, and nearly half are purchased by women.

139. The shelf-life of a latex condom is about two years.

140. Latex condoms can be rendered virtually ineffective as protection from STDs when used with a petroleum-based product such as Vaseline or mineral oil. Use of such products causes rapid deterioration of latex, resulting in minute perforations through which viral and bacterial contaminates may enter.

141. Women who use birth control pills should consult their doctor or pharmacist before taking an antibiotic. Some antibiotic

drug therapies may lessen the effectiveness of oral contraceptives.

142. The most effective form of female contraception is sterilization (100 percent), and also the most popular, with over one third of married women in the United States choosing it as a means of birth control. The least effective is douching, with a failure rate of up to forty percent.

143. Over 110 billion Tampax tampons have been sold since 1936.

144. Female contraceptives are sold in 20 percent of U.S. grocery stores.

145. Reporter Walter Winchell was said to employ any means to obtain a story, including the use of a car equipped with a police radio, red light, and siren. It's claimed that Lucille Ball first received confirmation of her pregnancy while listening to a Winchell broadcast—information obtained by Winchell from lab informants who called him before notifying her doctor.

146. Television censorship during the 1950s prohibited the word "pregnant" to be aired on the "I Love Lucy" show during the very visible real-life pregnancy of its star, Lucille Ball.

147. On December 2, 1952, viewers of the "March of Medicine" show witnessed the first televised birth of a baby. A five-pound, seven-ounce son delivered by cesarian section to Lillian Kerr of Denver, Colorado, was shown on over forty-nine NBC affiliates nationwide.

148. Edith Bunker, character of the seventies' sitcom "All in the Family," was the first female to experience menopause on T.V.

149. Television viewers are exposed to some form of sexual representation about twelve times per hour—or every five minutes.

150. On November 1, 1968, the Motion Picture Association of America (MPAA) created the "X" rating for excessively violent or sexually explicit films.

151. Long before the MPAA began rating its movies, the Catholic Legion of Decency had, since 1933, provided censorship for films in the form of an A, B, or C rating code. An "A" rating was approved for all ages; a "B" rating required discretion, and a "C" rating, reserved for films that displayed even a hint of nudity, sex, or suggestive language, meant "condemned for all ages." The legion was said to have wielded considerable influence on the moviegoing habits of its ten million members as well as the general public; influence that ultimately extended to the movie industry itself.

152. The movie *Midnight Cowboy*, winner of the "Best Picture" Academy Award in 1969, received an "X" rating from the Motion Picture Association when it was first released.

153. Cancer of the penis accounts for 1 to 2 percent of all male cancers; cancer of the prostate, 20 percent. Cancer of the testes has the best survival rate among male cancers (89 percent after five years).

154. There has long been a persistent rumor that the diminutive (one-inch) severed penis of Napoleon Bonaparte was sold to an American urologist in 1977 for $3,800. Similar claims have been made about the penises of Russian Grigori Rasputin and gangster John Dillinger, both of whom were said to have been overly endowed. In Rasputin's case, it was reported that his thirteen-inch blackened penis was kept for many years by his maid in a wooden box.

155. The notorious "Plaster Casters" of the 1960s were rock groupies who allegedly made plaster molds of their idols' penises. The late Jimi Hendrix was said to have enthusiastically complied with requests to immortalize his penis in plaster.

156. Adolph Hitler was rumored to have been born with only one testicle.

157. It is claimed that Ann Boleyn, second wife of Henry VIII, possessed the physical anomalies of an extra digit on one hand, and a third breast.

158. *Boyd's Book of Odd Facts* reports that one out of every two hundred women is endowed with an extra nipple.

159. When selecting a potential romantic partner, physical attractiveness is more important to men than women. A Yale study involving 2,247 personal ads found that men were twice as likely as women to seek a respondent who was physically attractive. In a similar study by the University of New Mexico, over 33 percent of men requested a "slim" partner, whereas only 2 percent of women deemed it important.

160. Prior to the silicone breast implant scandal, a surgical breast augmentation procedure was performed every minute in 1988 (that's over 525,500 a year), at an average cost of $3,500 per procedure.

161. Few black or ethnic minority women surgically enlarge their breasts; 98.5 percent of breast augmentation surgery is performed on Caucasian women.

162. The U.S. Center for Health Statistics reports that 2 percent of silicone breast implants are performed on men.

163. Margaret Gorman, winner of the first Miss America pageant (1921) held in Atlantic City, New Jersey, had a thirty-inch bust.

164. The 1985 "America in the Eighties" market research, by RH Bruskin Associates, discovered that 20 percent of American women have a bust measurement greater than thirty-seven inches, while a similar 1970 survey revealed that 20 percent have a measurement of less than thirty-two inches.

165. Over half of American mothers breastfeed their babies.

166. A new mother who breastfeeds her baby for six months will produce about 225 liters of milk—that's over fifty-six gallons.

167. Alfred Goldson, inventor of the "Baby Bonder" bib, has sold over 5,000 of the artificial terrycloth "breasts" which hold a baby bottle and can be strapped onto the chest. Goldson devised his bib so that new fathers could experience the joy of "breast-feeding" their baby.

168. Breast cancer is the most prevalent female cancer (27 percent), and has a survival rate of 74 percent after five years. The least deadly female malignancy is cancer of the uterus (10 percent occurrence), which has a survival rate of 83 percent after five years.

169. George Jorgensen, a former American G.I. who acquired fame in 1950 by undergoing sex-change surgery to become "Christine," was not the first transsexual to successfully reassign his gender. The first documented case was Danish artist Andreas Sparrer, who, in 1930, became Lili Elbe.

170. The periodical publication *Transition* is dedicated to transsexuals and transvestites, offering supportive articles and advice on such subjects as deportment, flattering fashions, and makeup tips.

171. Over two hundred Americans have sex-change surgery annually.

172. Among transsexuals who choose sex-change surgery, females who elect to become male are reported to be happier and better adjusted postoperatively than males who undergo surgery to become female.

173. Over seven hundred same-sex marriages have been performed in Denmark since 1989, when it became the first country to legally permit such unions.

174. Surveillance of Acquired Immune Deficiency Syndrome (AIDS) began in 1981. As of November 1991, 199,417 cases of the disease were diagnosed in the United States, and of that number, 128,857 have resulted in death. Nearly 25 percent of the total cases diagnosed since 1981 occurred between December 1990 and November 1991. The World Health Organization estimates between 2 to 5 million persons may be infected globally.

175. Over 3,600 American children age thirteen or younger have been infected with the AIDS virus from sources other than birth. Of that number, 2500* were infected by intravenous drug use or sexual contact.

176. The oldest documented case of an AIDS-related death occurred in 1959. Diagnostic tests performed on preserved tissue samples of a twenty-five-year-old sailor from Manchester, England, who died of a mysterious illness, were confirmed in 1990 to be infected with the AIDS virus.

177. Worldwide, the most common mode of transmission of the HIV virus is through heterosexual intercourse (60 percent).

178. Although women infected with the AIDS virus comprise 10 percent of the total number of cases, their survival time from diagnosis until death is one-tenth that of white gay AIDS-infected men (an average 15.5 weeks for women, compared to 156 weeks for a gay white male). In New York City, AIDS is the leading cause of death among women between the ages of twenty-five and thirty-four.

179. The greatest number of AIDS-related deaths in the United States occur among persons between the ages of thirty and thirty-nine, and accounted for over 45 percent of such deaths in 1989. Ninety percent of AIDS deaths that year were men.

180. Every twelve minutes in the United States someone is

*These are reported cases to the CDC. Actual figures may be much higher.

infected with the AIDS virus, and every thirty minutes there is an AIDS-related death.

181. Cuba is the only nation to require mandatory testing of its citizens for the AIDS virus. Those testing positive for the disease are sent to a special quarantine center in Havana to segregate them from the healthy population. Foreigners entering the country are also required by the Cuban government to be tested for AIDS.

182. Over 60 percent of all AIDS victims worldwide are living in Africa.

183. On September 21, 1989, a Tennessee woman, Mary Sue Davis, was awarded temporary custody of seven frozen embryos after she and her husband, Junior, decided to divorce. The custody battle ensued after a disagreement arose over ownership and use of the embryos.

184. Of the 25,744 attempts to conceive in 1990 by couples receiving treatment at fertility clinics, only 3,951 resulted in successful pregnancy and delivery of a baby.

185. Worried about inflation? Take heart. Nowhere, except at your local sperm bank, can you buy so much for so little. At an average cost of $100, you can purchase up to 100,000,000 sperm (that's 1,000,000 sperm per dollar, or 10,000 for a penny). Now that's a bargain!

186. Commercial sperm banks pay screened donors an average of $50 per specimen.

187. Some 20,000 to 60,000 babies born each year were conceived with donor sperm.

188. Sperm banks keep donor semen frozen at approximately −321 degrees Fahrenheit and properly preserved specimens can be kept indefinitely. There has been documented use of sixteen-year-old semen, which resulted in the birth of a normal child.

189. Dr. R. G. Bunge, of the University of Iowa, was credited in 1953 with the first human birth resulting from artificial insemination of frozen semen.

190. Since 1980 over one thousand babies have been born to surrogate mothers.

191. Surrogate mothers were an accepted practice in ancient Rome. Male heirs were prized, and high infant mortality and/or infertility often made it necessary to seek help from a female family friend who was willing to be impregnated by the husband and produce a child for the barren couple to raise as their own.

192. Surrogate mothers are usually paid a fee of between $10,000 to $12,000 for a successful pregnancy and delivery.

193. Parents who use the services of a surrogate mother will typically pay about $30,000 to $40,000 for medical and legal fees. That figure may be much higher if the couple wishes to implant the surrogate with their frozen embryo—about $5,000 per implantation procedure.

194. British gynecologist Patrick Steptoe pioneered the procedure for in vitro fertilization in the 1970s.

195. The first "test tube" baby born by IVF (in vitro fertilization) was five-pound, 12-ounce Louise Brown, born July 25, 1978, to thirty-one-year-old Lesley Brown, of Manchester, England. Elizabeth Carr, born December 8, 1981, in Norfolk, Virginia, was the first American IVF baby.

196. A fifty-two-year-old Californian, Joni Mosby Mitchell, gave birth to a son in April 1992 to become the oldest American mother to have a baby by IVF. Postmenopausal, she was successfully implanted with an embryo conceived with a donor egg and her husband's sperm.

197. The 1986 Attorney General's Commission on Pornography reported that porn actors of X-rated movies received an average salary of $350 to $500 per day, and that "porn stars" earned

$1,000 to $2,500 per day. Some film companies pay performers per sex act—the amount determined by the type and number of sex acts performed.

198. The eleven-member Attorney General's commission reviewed 5,470 items of sexually oriented material (2,375 magazines, 725 books, and 2,370 movies).

199. Trivia columnist L. M. Boyd claims that "adult" bookstores outnumber McDonald's restaurants three to one.

200. "Dial-A-Porn" service began in 1982 with the advent of telephone deregulation and is now a $2.4 billion industry. Some phone-sex companies can transmit as many as fifty thousand sexually explicit messages per hour, and it's estimated that over forty thousand such calls are made daily.

201. The telephone company receives up to $.19 for one minute of Dial-A-Porn service. Pacific Bell estimated that in 1985 it earned $12 million from phone sex.

202. There are over thirty-six different varieties of flowers which express sentiments of attraction, love, or passion, and more than fifteen that convey negative feelings. Beware of a bouquet containing yellow carnations, chrysanthemums, hyacinth, and roses, along with a few marigolds, hydrangea, petunias, and orange lilies. The giver may be saying, among other things, that you are fickle, cruel, deceitful, unloving, frigid, heartless, jealous, and hateful.

203. The Feast of Lupercalia, an ancient Roman celebration held every February 15th in dedication to the fertility god Lupercus and goddess of love, Venus, featured a "lottery" where eligible bachelors could draw from a large urn the name of a young maiden to court. Valentine's Day was said to have evolved from this ancient Roman feast day.

204. American Greetings Company states that Valentine's Day is the second largest card-giving holiday, with over 1 billion

cards exchanged annually—although it's teachers, not sweethearts and lovers, who receive the most cards.

205. In their lifetime, Americans will fall in love an average of six times, and will have approximately seven different sexual partners.

206. The average American divorcée was married seven years before ending the union.

207. Readers of romance novels have sex more frequently than readers of any other genre.

208. The "Empathy Belly," a patented device invented by a Washington childbirth instructor, allows the wearer to experience over twenty symptoms of pregnancy. A tight binder for the ribs causes shortness of breath and heartburn; a large canvas sack filled with eleven pounds of warm water simulates the increased weight of the abdomen, and a pouch containing six pounds of lead buckshot is placed over the lower abdomen to create constant pressure on the bladder. The device also comes complete with a two-pound swinging pendulum to mimic baby's kicking.

209. Approximately every minute in the United States there are four marriages, seven births, and two divorces.

210. A person who collects trivia is known as a "spermologer."

ANSWERS TO THE SEXUAL TRIVIA CHALLENGE

1. B. 4 inches

2. B. 4 inches

3. A. 5 calories

4. B. 100 calories

5. A. 300 sperm

6. C. China—they have developed an oral contraceptive using Gossypol, a derivative of cottonseed oil, which is thought to be an effective metabolic spermicide.

7. C. a hickey

8. C. chocolate

9. A. eyes—Tincture of belladonna was used as an eye drop to dilate the pupil, making the eyes darker, and in contrast, the complexion lighter.

10. C. naked

11. A. *Maraichinage* is named for the Maraichins of Brittany, France, who customarily exchanged prolonged deep tongue kisses.

12. B. $.50

13. A. Nuns—a brothel was referred to as a "nunnery."

14. C. oral contraceptives

15. B. Marquis de Sade

16. C. King Louis XV shipped prostitutes and criminals from his women's prison to New Orleans.

17. B. Soiled clothes that carry the scent of a loved one and can be sniffed when the wearer is absent.

18. A. polygyny (a male with multiple wives)

19. C. India—the Toda society has no word for adultery in its vocabulary, and extramarital lovers are permitted.

20. A. Ireland—the inhabitants of Inis Beag, off the Irish coast, are ignorant of even basic sexual physiology, and female orgasm is virtually unknown.

21. A. "eating penises"

22. A. rhinoceros horn, and B. black bear gallbladder
    *If you guessed both, take an extra point.

23. C. Jimmy Carter—born 1924 at Wise Sanitarium in Plains, Georgia

24. C. infibulating (suturing) her genitals

25. B. a lover of women

26. A. stolen women's panties

27. C. 22—The Yates sisters must have had fun!

28. A. Alaska, and C. Utah
    *Take an extra point if you guessed both.

29. B. 1987—Television station KRON of San Francisco aired the first condom commercial on January 16 of that year.

30. C. 25 percent

31. B. 25 percent

32. A. heterosexual intercourse

33. A. Denmark—over 700 legal same-sex marriages have been performed since 1989.

34. B. Africa

35. B. 7 years

36. C. rock groupies who made plaster molds of their idol's penises

How Did You Score?

0–9 correct. Sorry! (You need a remedial course in Sex 101.)

10–18 correct. Better! (Do you own a polyester leisure suit? Black vinyl thigh-top boots? If you answered "yes" to **both** questions, you should seek the services of a sex therapist.)

19–27 correct. Not bad! (If you scored more than 50 percent correct, you did better than the 1,974 adults who took the 1989 Kinsey Institute test of basic sexual knowledge.)

28–36 correct. Sexpert! (We know what you do with your spare time.)

SOURCES

American Greetings Corp., Cleveland, Ohio.

The American Heritage Dictionaries, eds. *Word Mysteries & Histories: From Quiche to Humble Pie*. Boston: Houghton Mifflin Company, 1986.

Angeloni, Elvio, ed. *Anthropology Today 88/89*. Guilford, Conn.: Dushkin Publishing Group, 1986.

Aries, Phillippe, and George Duby. *A History of Private Life*. Vol. 1, *From Pagan Rome to Byzantium*, Vol. 2, *Revelations of the Medieval World*. Vol. 4 *From the Fires of the Revolution to the Great War*. Camebridge, Mass.: Harvard University Press, 1987, 1988, 1990.

Atkins, Thomas, ed. *Sexuality in the Movies*. Indiana: Indiana University Press, 1975.

The Attorney General's Commission on Pornography Report. Nashville, Tenn.: Rutledge Hill Press, 1986.

Biracree, Tom, and Nancy. *Almanac of the American people*. New York: Facts on File, 1988.

Boyd, L. M. *Boyd's Book of Odd Facts*. New York: New American Library, 1979.

———. *Boyd's Curiosity Shop*. New York: Dell Publishing, 1986.

Bullough, Vern L., and Bonnie. *Sin, Sickness, & Sanity: A History of Sexual Attitudes*. New York and London: Garland Publishing, 1977.

Center for Surrogate Parenting, Inc. 8383 Wilshire Boulevard, Beverly Hills, California.

Coleman, James C. *Intimate Relationships, Marriage, and Family*. New York: Macmillan, 1985.

Danforth, David, ed. *Obstetrics and Gynecology*. New York: Harper & Row, 1977.

Demarest, Robert J., and John J. Sciarra M.D. *Conception, Birth and Contraception—A Visual Presentation*. New York: McGraw-Hill, 1969.

Ellis, Albert, and Albert Abarbanel. *The Encyclopedia of Sexual Behavior*. New York: Jason Aronson, 1973.

D'Emillio, John, and Estelle Freedman. *Intimate Matters—A History of Sexuality in America*. New York: Harper & Row.

Endleman, Robert. *Love and Sex in Twelve Cultures*. New York: Psyche Press, 1989.

Fabulous Fallacies. New York: Harmony Books, 1982.

Firkin, B. G., and J. A. Whitworth. *Dictionary of Medical Eponyms*. Park Ridge, N.J.: Parthenon Publishing Co., 1990.

Ford, C. S., and F. A. Beach. *Patterns of Sexual Behavior*. Westport, Conn.: Greenwood Press, 1951.

Francoer, Robert T. *A Descriptive Dictionary and Atlas of Sexology*. New York: Greenwood Press, 1991.

Fraser, Harrison. *The Dark Angel—Aspects of Victorian Sexuality*. New York: Universal Books, 1978.

Frayser, Suzanne G. *Varieties of Sexual Experience*. New Haven, Conn.: HRAF Press, 1985.

Gonzalez-Crussi, F. *On the Nature of Things Erotic*. San Diego, Calif.: Harcourt Brace Jovanovich, 1988.

Good Housekeeping's Women's Almanac. 1977.

HIV/AIDS Surveillance 1992. Centers for Disease Control, Washington, D.C.: U.S. Dept. of Health and Human Services, 1992.

Heyman, Tom. *On an Average Day*. New York: Ballantine, 1989.

Hopson, Janet. *Scent Signals*. William Morrow, 1979.

Information Please Almanac, 1990: The New Universe of Information, Information Please Almanic, 1992: The New Universe of Information. Boston: Houghton Mifflin Co., 1990, 1992.

Johns, Catherine. *Sex or Symbol—Erotic Images of Greece and Rome*. Austin, Texas: University of Texas Press, 1982.

Johnson, Warren R. *Human Sex and Sex Education—Perspectives and Problems*. Malvern, Penn.: Lea & Febigel, 1963.

Kay, Margarita Artschwager, R.N., Ph.D. *Anthropology of Human Birth*. Philadelphia: F. A. Davis, 1982.

Keuls, Eva C. *The Reign of the Phallus—Sexual Politics in Ancient Athens*. New York: Harper and Row, 1978.

Lanson, M.D., Luciene. *From Woman to Woman—A Gynecologist Answers Questions About Your Body*. New York: Knopf, 1975.

Lapham, Lewis H. et al. *Harper's Index*. New York: Henry Holt and Co., 1991.

Lewinsohn, Richard. *A History of Sexual Customs*. New York: Longman, Green, and Co., and Harper & Brothers, 1958.

MacNamara, Donald E. J., and Edward Sayarin. *Sex, Crime, and the Law*. New York: Free Press, 1977.

Marshall, Donald S., and Suggs, Robert C., ed. *Human Sexual Behavior—Variations in the Ethnographic Spectrum*. New York: Basic Books, 1971.

Masters and Johnson. *On Sex and Human Loving. Human Sexual Response*. New York: Little, Brown & Co., 1966, 1982.

Malinowski, Bronislaw. *The Sexual Life of Savages*. New York: Harcourt, Brace & World, 1929.

McFarlan, Donald, ed· *The 1992 Guinness Book of World Records.* New York: Bantam Books, 1992.

McLaren, Angus. *A History of Contraception: From Antiquity to Present Day*. Cambridge, Mass.: Basil Blackwell, 1990.

Mohr, James C. *Abortion in America: The Origins and Evolution of National Policy, 1800-1900*. New York: Oxford University Press, 1978.

Money, John. *The Destroying Angel—Sex, Fitness & Food in the Legacy of Degeneracy Theory, Graham Crackers, Kellogg's Corn Flakes & and American Health History*. New York. Prometheus Books, 1985.

Murphy, Emmett. *The Great Bordellos of the World*. London: Quartet Books, 1983.

Murstein, Bernard I. *Love, Sex, & Marriage Through the Ages*. New York: Springer, 1974.

Newman, Art. *The Illustrated Treasury of Medical Curiosa*. New York: McGraw-Hill, 1988.

Poretz, Mel, and Barry Sinrod. *Do You do it with the Lights On?* New York: Ballantine, 1991.

Porter, Valerie. *The Guinness Book of Marriage*. Mill Valley, Calif.: Guinness Publishing, 1991.

Reinisch, June, Ph.D., and Ruth Beasley M.L.S. *The Kinsey Institute New Report On Sex*. New York: St. Martin's Press, 1990.

Reuben, M.D., David, *Everything You Always Wanted to Know About Sex* but were afraid to ask*.

Sexually Transmitted Disease Surveillance 1990. Atlanta, Ga.: U.S. Dept. Health and Human Services, 1990.

Smith, Bradley. *The American Way of Sex*. La Jolla, Calif.: Gemini Smith, 1978.

Statistical Abstract of the United States 1991: The National Data Book. Washington, D.C.: U.S. Department of Commerce, 1991.

STD Statistics. Atlanta, Ga.: U.S. Deaprtment of Health and Human Services, Centers for Disease Control, 1990.

Symanski, Richard. *The Immoral Landscape—Female Prostitution in Western Societies*. Stoneham, Mass.: Butterworth, 1981.

Taylor, G. Rattay. *Sex in History*. New York: Vanguard Press, 1954.

Tuleja, Tad. *Curious Customs*. New York: Harmony Books, 1987.

U.S. Department of Justice, Uniform Crime Report 1990. Federal Bureau of Investigation, Washington D.C., 1990.

Vanoni, Marvin. *I've Got Goose Pimples: Our Great Expressions and How They Came to Be*. New York: William Morrow, 1989.

Wallace, Irving. *The Nympho and other Maniacs*. New York: Simon & Schuster, 1971.

Wallace, Irving, and Amy, Sylvia, and David Wallechinsky. *The Intimate Sex Lives of Famous People*. New York: Delacorte Press, 1981.

Wallechinsky and Wallace. *Peoples Almanac 3*. New York: William Morrow, 1981.

Wallechinsky, Wallace, and Wallace. *The Book of Lists*, *The Book of Lists 2*, and *The Book of Lists 3*. New York: William Morrow, 1977.

Weiss, Daniel Evan. *100% American*. New York: Poseidon Press, 1988.

The World Almanac & Book of Facts 1991. World Almanac & Book of Facts Staff, eds. New York: Pharohs Books, 1991.

Wright, John W., ed. *The Universal Almanac 1990*, and *The Universal Almanac 1992*. Missouri: Universal Press Syndicate, 1990, 1992.